The Complete
Bonnie August's
Dress Thin System

The Complete
Bonnie August's
Dress Thin System

642 + Ways
to Correct Figure Faults
with Clothes

with Ellen Count

Rawson, Wade Publishers, Inc.

NEW YORK

Library of Congress Cataloging in Publication Data

August, Bonnie.
   The complete bonnie august dress thin system
   Includes index.
   1. Clothing and dress.   2. Fashion.   I. Count,
Ellen, joint author.   II. Title.
TT507.A83   646'34   80–51245
ISBN 0–89256–137–8

Illustrated by Bonnie August
Illustration layout by Carl Van Brunt
Designed by Jacques Chazaud

First Edition

To our Body Type prototypes
with affection

Lee Miles	Anne Gayler
Dale Corsello	Meredith Bernstein
Ann Williamson	Maxine Davidowitz
Raeanne Rubenstein	Mary Zakany

Ellen Sideri

And to a host of others who generously provided aid and comfort to the authors:

Penney Dante, Carl Van Brunt, D. J. White, Marylou Luther, Arthur Imparato, Gemma Insinna, Edith Head, Suzy Kalter, Jean Hill, Jo Whitlow, Alexander Julian, Robert E. Brown, Robyrta Rapoport, Eleanor Fobert

Bernard Vidal, Michelle Stevens, Anthony Accardo, Frances Pellegrini, Sylvia Massey, Charles F. Stuckey, Andrea Fonyo

Ralph August, Gertrude August, Marilyn August, Ruth Count, Sibyl Count, Donald C. Waterman, Eleanor Rawson, Martin Manasse, Patricia Tregellas, Warren Pelton, Dorothy Harper, Philip Friedman, Charles Butera, Laurie Scandurra, Carol Gladstone, Yann Weymouth, Lillian Friedman, Allan J. Berlowitz

We also gratefully acknowledge the contributions made by the fashion experts and creators and other authorities who are quoted in these pages.

Contents

Introduction
Behind the Dress Thin System . . .
My Body/Style Philosophy

One of the reasons my Dress Thin System works is that from the time I started designing when I was nineteen, I have always created clothes not just to be esthetically pleasing in themselves, but to *complement the body*—especially the body in motion. Having been involved in active sports ever since high school, I gravitated naturally to a body-aware vision of fashion. And in recent years, the experience of designing Danskins not just for dancing but for all the sports I've enjoyed myself—swimming, running, tennis, gymnastics, skiing and skating—served to crystallize the philosophy behind the system of dressing you'll learn from this book.

Important to the System, of course, are the artist's fundamentals of proportion and illusion which I learned at Syracuse University, where I majored in fabric design at the School of Fine Arts. It was also there that—inspired by the first fashion professional I ever met and one of the most creative, Syracuse graduate Betsey Johnson—I began to consider a career in fashion.

After graduation, my design assignments led off with close-to-the-body ski underwear, and worked out from there. I created ski clothes for Aspen Skiwear and for White Stag; designed my own signature scarf line, and print fabrics for fashion interiors. I also designed Art Déco costume jewelry which sometimes turns up in antiques shops where it is sold as the real thing! I did freelance fashion illustration, too, and some of my paintings were as tall as real models—maybe taller. Working constantly with models themselves, I watched the best ones combine their knowledge of fashion and of their own proportions with their personalities to express what I came to think of as their individual concepts of Body/Style.

When I joined Danskin in 1975, I began to design for dancers, the most proportion-conscious women of all, and found in leotards the ideal fashion medium for my Body/Style philosophy. Bodywear, I quickly realized, need not be reserved only for dancers but would work perfectly for the increasingly active lives of most American women. The logical next step: multipurpose leotards that could go to the beach as easily as to the ballet *barre*. Then, after I added graceful wrap skirts to match, they were also worn on the street and to all the best discos in the prime of their popularity. Meantime, tennis players, skaters and gymnasts wore Danskins that I designed especially for them.

I must admit that my timing couldn't have been better. The 1960s had liberated women to enjoy "wearing" their bodies as never before. . . . In the '70s, they wore my Danskin designs while they exercised to improve what they had—and then to show off the great results.

When American Ballet Theatre ballerina Rebecca Wright became a consultant to Danskin, I saw through a dancer's eyes the streamlining effect that practice clothes can have on the body when properly designed. Rebecca Wright always emphasized that one close-up look in the mirror is not enough to evaluate what you're wearing. "*First,* stand close to a full-length mirror, look for details and correct them," she explained. "Then be sure to move back and get a long view of yourself. It's essential to analyze your proportions and make adjustments from that perspective, too."

As I accompanied Becky to ballet classes and rehearsals, I observed how dancers use dark or light shades to camouflage body flaws or highlight assets . . . how they manipulate necklines to accent breast curves, and leglines to elongate their limbs. (I'll show you in Part Two, Chapter 1, how *you* can adapt dancers' costume savvy to solve your swimwear problems.)

Most important of all, from my contact with dancers, gymnasts and skaters, I absorbed their expertise at playing with their proportions in order to emphasize their best features and downplay the rest. A dancer has to be a body connoisseur. By knowing everything about her body from every angle, she knows just where to make her audience focus to remember the very best of her. Use my System—and you'll be able to do exactly the same!

From then on, I know you will shop (or sew) without the sad, expensive mistakes that end up in the backs of closets and drawers. What's more, I'm sure you'll enjoy counting the *dollars you save*—instead of the calories you deny yourself—as you seem to lose pounds painlessly with my Dress Thin System: the fashion system I designed to solve figure problems like yours . . . problems every woman I know confronts in the mirror every day.

B. A.

PART ONE

The Designer Dress Thin System

You don't need willpower to Dress Thin

We've all dieted and we've all exercised—or tried—and I admit I'm no exception. I haven't found either route to figure improvement any easier than you have. Sometimes I've been resolute enough to make both work, sometimes not. But I have discovered something that *always* works—without self-control! So if you can't seem to muster the willpower to follow a tough regime—or even if your bone structure just wasn't *built* thin—you'll find you can still *dress* thin with the versatile fun-to-learn proportion-correcting system I designed for, and with, my friends.

You'll also find that there are things you can accomplish with my System—illusions you can create—that *no* diet or exercise routine can achieve. (Did you ever read a diet or exercise remedy for broad shoulders?)

You needn't sweat to learn my Dress Thin System or to use it well. Nor do you have to worry about your mouth and what you put into it. All I'm going to ask you to do is open your mind and, above all, your eyes. Compared to changing your lifetime eating patterns, learning to *really* look at yourself in the mirror is not only a breeze, but will even be fun.

To put my System to work for you, you'll need a willingness to discard many preconceptions about your figure, plus plenty of curiosity about how clothes can change your look. That's where that mirror I just mentioned comes in. If you don't already own a good one—full length, without distorting flaws—you *must* get hold of one, now. Among other revelations, it will soon show you what has made some of your clothes all-time favorites and why others were never right for you from the day you brought them home.

1

A technique instead of a mystique

At just about the time I started to write this book, I suddenly realized that the world had gone cooking crazy. But I also noticed that before they began investing in extravagant new stew pots and crêpe pans, all those cooking-crazed types headed straight to the bookstores for cookbooks to help them put it all together properly.

Most of the very same women who believe that cooking well is a skill that one must learn assured me (when I could get them to turn off the food processor for a minute) that *dressing* well is some sort of instinct that one either is born with or must manage forever without. But that's the delightful difference between them—and those of you who have picked up this book. If you have always harbored a hope or a hunch that just as a cookbook could help you cook better, a dressing book could help you look better in the clothes you wear, you're right!

And here's your hunch come true: a "recipe" approach to proportion-corrected dressing that will improve your image as soon as you begin to use it. In a unique, systematic way, I'm about to help you substitute reliable dressing techniques for the confusing fashion mystique that's prevailed until now. And my Dress Thin recipes are all based on the essential ingredient—*your* figure.

You'll start by getting a new visual understanding of your figure, head to toe. Once you've got it, you'll never again have to rely on hit-or-miss guesswork when you decide you want a new dress or even a pair of shoes. And then you'll discover how to stir in those wonderful intangibles—your personality and your lifestyle—to spice up your dressing in a satisfying new way.

Not that you'll have it all down pat after one quick reading, any more than you could cook everything in the cookbook from memory the second time around. But when you need a new suit, for instance, you'll reach for my master plan and review Chapter 5, "Dress Thin Power Plays," just the way you'd bone up on ragouts if you were in the market for a new stew.

The idea that's been my inspiration—and your hunch—is just this: Exactly as you'd learn to cook, you can learn to dress in proportion with your figure, given some basic techniques, some practice and a good reference book to give you a refresher any time you need one. And I do mean any time. Unlike other dressing books, this one is not based on trends that will date next season. You can go on consulting the pages of my Dress Thin Style Guide for years and continue to find illustrations that relate to clothes on the market at any point in the fashion cycle.

As for the mystique of "instinctive" dressing, let's replace it with the idea that the better your *technique* is, the more creative you can be. You weren't born dressed, but you can *learn* to choose your clothes intelligently for your body and wear them with personal flair. And eliminate once and for all the guesswork that usually results in expensive clothes mistakes.

See yourself in proportion and Dress Thin

When I conceived the idea of a Dress Thin System, my main concern was for the *visual* proportions that make clothes look better on the body. But as I began to research my book in earnest, I soon understood that the *psychological* meaning of the phrase "sense of proportion" is important to my System, too. Because before you can learn a new way to see how you look in clothes, you need an inner sense of proportion about your body that few of us have.

We're too accustomed to dwelling on our figure faults as just that: faults. We agonize about them and blame ourselves, as if we really were somehow *at fault* for being too large here or too small there. The upshot is that most of us *literally* can't see ourselves clearly enough to make a few useful corrections with our *clothes*—instead of wasting time on a lot of unproductive value judgments that come out of our heads. And what about the blind spots that prevent us from recognizing our all-important figure *assets*?

I suppose I always have known that women are this way. After all, even the tall, thin models I meet at work are constantly criticizing their bodies. But it was on a special Sunday afternoon that I understood how our value judgments can get in the way of precisely the clear-eyed assessments that actually can help.

I had asked a dozen women friends to put on leotards and spend that afternoon as my Body Type prototypes. For each one, I made a Proportion Pattern, described on p. 4. As I drew their patterns, I questioned my friends about their figures and their clothes, and tape-recorded their comments and questions. "I think my legs are too short for my body but I'm not sure. Am I long-waisted?" and more . . .

But there was one friend, a five-foot-two fashion consultant who seemed to see her body in proportion, both visually and psychologically. Something she said that day expresses the idea behind the Dress Thin System. I think it will inspire you as it did me. . . .

"For years, I spent so much time worrying about all the things that were 'wrong.' I never spent any time figuring out how to correct them. But I finally came to a point where I realized that nobody measures attraction—even physical attraction— with a tape measure. And nobody ever ran screaming from the room when I took off my clothes, either. So, eventually you do reach a certain level of psychological self-support—a certain acceptance. One day it hits you that being loved isn't a matter of ten pounds more or ten pounds less. Then I learned to stop focusing on being five feet two inches and chunky, and to think this is what I am—what can I do? How can I make myself look as thin as possible with what I wear?

"If you can come to know yourself, you can see yourself objectively . . . okay, I'm never going to be five foot six and have thin legs or thin hips. Now—how can I compensate with clothes?

"Well, there is a kind of balance—it's a visual effect, an illusion—I'm learning to create for myself. And it really is something that can be learned!"

Make your Proportion Pattern and never second-guess your figure again!

That friend was one of many fashion experts who assured me that *with a good system,* anyone could learn very quickly an approach to dressing that ordinarily takes years of practice to perfect. Their encouragement led to my Proportion Pattern, the Squint Trick, the Body Type alphabet and Body Signs that all together comprise the Dress Thin System you're about to learn.

To make your Proportion Pattern—the first step in learning my System—all you need are a roll of brown wrapping paper large enough to draw your body on it full-size twice, obtainable at your variety store (the label on the one we used says 2½' x 4 yards 2'), a yardstick and two felt-tip markers. Get markers in any bright color that will show up well on your wrapping paper. One should be fairly thin, to make a line ¹/₁₆ inch to ⅛ inch wide; the other should have the broadest tip you can find. You'll also need a friend who wants to learn the Dress Thin System, too. Both of you should wear leotards* when you make your Proportion Patterns.

As you'll see, your Proportion Pattern is a visual aid to help you get a new perspective on your body. It completely eliminates any distasteful bouts with a tape measure. You may take a couple of novel measurements with your yardstick, but you'll use it most for drawing straight lines on your Pattern. I deliberately designed this process so you can learn my System without undergoing the kind of tape-measure trauma that makes many of us discouraged about our bodies, instead of interested in them and eager to discover new ways of looking at and dressing them. With the Proportion Pattern, you'll find that what's important is not how many inches this or that part of you measures, but the *proportion* of certain parts to others.

Now, here are the five simple steps it will take to make your Proportion Pattern, front view and profile:

1. Lie down on your back on a sheet of the wrapping paper with your head near the top and your feet near the bottom. Position yourself as far to one side of the paper as you can and not have any part of you off the paper. Your heels should be together and your hands two inches away from your sides. (Be prepared to lie still for a few minutes.)

2. Your friend should use the thinner marker to draw around you, tracing the outline of your body from head to heels. After she has drawn your outline, open your legs enough so that she can put a mark on the pattern at the crotch point—where your legs and torso meet. While drawing, the marker should be *right next to your body,* held in a *straight-up-and-down* position, not slanted as for writing. This helps assure that you get a reasonably "true" outline rather than one that's a lot smaller than your body actually is. When your friend has finished your front view outline, it's your turn to draw hers.

---

*Not shorts. If you don't own leotards, second best are bra and panties.

3. Next, if wall space permits, tape the two sheets of paper next to each other on a wall (otherwise, tape one on an unpaneled door), making sure that the top of the paper is a few inches above your respective heads. If space is limited, hang one sheet at a time.

4. Now, each of you in turn will draw the other from one side (it doesn't matter whether you choose right or left) using the empty space next to your front view drawing. Stand sideways, as straight as you can, with your side touching the wall. Raise the arm that's next to the wall and don't bother to draw it beyond the middle of the upper arm. Be sure, again, to do the drawings with the marker held upright and right next to the body. *IMPORTANT:* in tracing the front and back of your profile view, be especially careful to follow each curve closely. Do *not* hold in that tummy but be sure to *record* it, and any midriff curve above it, faithfully on your Pattern. Also be absolutely sure to accurately record your derrière and bust curves, too.

5. Lastly, use the big felt-tip marker to color in your whole Proportion Pattern, both views. This is an essential step that gives you what you need to practice the Squint Trick.

The Squint Trick

Your Proportion Pattern actually functions like a new kind of mirror, so keep it taped up on the wall where you can see it easily. Unlike your mirror reflection, it won't move or get tired. And the Pattern profile view is a good substitute for the side view you can get only in a three-way mirror—a luxury few of us own. First we'll use the head-on Pattern to practice the Squint Trick. It's an ultra-simple way to begin understanding your proportions and I didn't even invent it! Every art student learns to use it when drawing from a model.

Fashion professionals use it constantly, almost unconsciously. In fact, as I was conferring one day with Sandra Karwoski, Education Director of Simplicity Pattern Company, and Simplicity's Editor of Instructional Books, Janet Du Bane, we realized that all of us depend on the Squint Trick, using it almost automatically to *suppress small details* and allow us to *see visual generalities* more easily.

Try it now with your Proportion Pattern. As you squint at it, ask yourself which major areas of your body seem to dominate the rest. Compare, for instance, the top of your body to the bottom: are you smaller above the waist than below? Or, do your legs appear to be short compared to your torso? About the same? The idea is to get general impressions—don't worry if you're not quite sure on the first try. You have already begun to sharpen your Dress Thin eye.

The more you practice this easy little trick, the more revealing you'll find it becomes. Soon you'll find yourself looking in the real mirror and using the Squint Trick to evaluate both the clothes you already own and potential new ones. In the next section, your Proportion Pattern will help you analyze your

Body Type and discover which of my Body Signs point right to the proportion-correcting clothes that make your personal Dress Thin System work.

Easy as A-b-d—the Body Type alphabet that helps you read your body

I'm tired of terms like "pearshape," which often are derogatory. Who wants to think of herself as a pear? Besides, there are several Body Types other than the pear, and everyone has difficulty describing them in a word or two. So, I devised a Body Type alphabet as a shorthand way to identify the various proportional imbalances that can all be corrected with clothes.

My alphabet has eleven lucky letters that will help you learn to "read" your body in a completely new way. In my alphabet, by the way, the letters aren't intended to stand for words; they are symbols for the way your body is shaped. Once you identify your Body Type initials, you'll find them as easy to remember as the initials that stand for your name.

You'll be able to put your Dress Thin System into action as soon as you identify your own Body Type and Body Signs, using your Proportion Pattern and the Four-step Body Type I.D. survey that's coming up. Most women are a combination of more than two types, so you will probably end up with a revealing group—a monogram!—of Body Type initials. You may recognize your figure in one or more of these initials on sight, but if you're at all uncertain, just follow my quick, easy directions to check your visual impression. The few minutes you spend will save you all the hours of time you'd normally waste on guessing what styles are most flattering to your figure—especially in fitting rooms.

You'll find that you can follow the Body Signs throughout my Dress Thin System Style Guide in Part II and quickly spot the styles that will work best for you. That's all it takes to pick up the proportion-correcting Dress Thin System basics.

Starting with the very first time you put yourself together this way, you'll look thinner—and better-dressed—faster than you ever thought possible. The more you practice, the better your Dress Thin eye will become—and the more it will do for your image.

Your Body Type and the Dress Thin Body Signs

The *key* to the Dress Thin System:

Understand your proportions with my simple Body Type I.D. survey.

Some of your Body Type initials may not be a surprise; others may reveal subtle proportion problems that clothes can easily correct and quickly produce a *major* change in your image. You may have from two to five initials in your Body Type monogram. The purpose of the Body Types is not to pigeonhole you, but to help pinpoint where proportional imbalances exist, eliminate guesswork and lay the foundation for your individual Dress Thin System.

The Body Type I.D. proportion survey that you're about to take identifies your Body Signs. Once you know them, you can follow the Style Guide recommendations in Part II of this book and begin to Dress Thin immediately. So right now, pin up your Proportion Pattern in full view and see how easy it is to check out your Body Type I.D.

Your Body Type I.D.

Never mind how anyone has described the shape you're in—your Proportion Pattern shows all! Clear your mind of preconceptions and visually compare your front view Pattern to the four primary Body Types shown here. Use the Squint Trick to see your Pattern clearly. Can you recognize the primary Body Type initial that looks most like you? If you're not positive, verifying your initial is as easy as connecting the dots. Just put your Proportion Pattern on the floor, get out your felt-tip marker and your yardstick and follow the notes underneath the initial that you suspect corresponds to the silhouette on your Pattern. *One of these four primary Body Types is you—Step One tells you which.* When you know your primary type, go right on to Step Two and see whether you should add a secondary initial to your Body Type monogram.

In using the Style Guide, be sure to follow my recommendations for ALL your initials. For instance, if your monogram is rT and a style that's recommended for r is a "Don't" for T . . . don't buy that style.

A Body Type I.D. short-cut method:

The reason the Proportion Pattern is the best way to learn your Body Type is that it makes objective evaluation easier for the many women who have trouble analyzing their figures the way a designer would. Suppose however, you're eager to discover your Body Type but choose not to make your Proportion Pattern. Try this short-cut method, always bearing in mind that unless you're objective you won't get the accurate results you need: wearing leotards, *face the full-length mirror straight on.* Instead of using the Squint Trick on your Proportion Pattern, *squint at your reflection.* Compare it one by one with the figures shown in Steps One through Three on the next four pages, and answer the questions below those figures. Then, standing at right angle to the mirror (this is not easy), use the Squint Trick on your profile reflection to compare your body with the figures shown in Step Four. As I've indicated, this is a second-best measure, but one that can be used successfully if you're brutally truthful in your self-appraisal.

STEP ONE: Are you an A, an X, an H or a V?

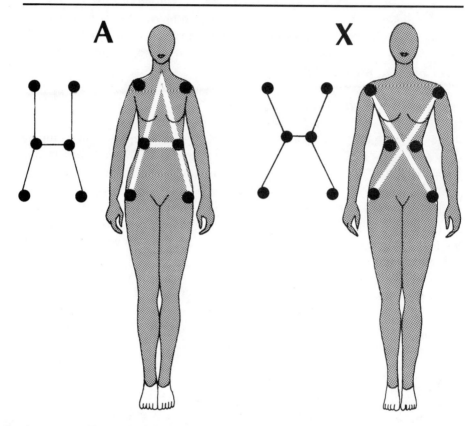

Squint at your Proportion Pattern. Do your shoulders look narrower than your thighs? Are you noticeably wider below the waist than above? Mark the shoulder, waist and thigh dots on your Pattern and connect them. If your dot diagram shapes up like this one, your primary Body Type is **A:** narrow above the waist, heavy below. But if it doesn't correspond, compare it with the other dot diagrams and see which of the three it most closely resembles. (If you're not **A,** try **X** next; then **H, V.**)

If **A** is your Body Type, look for that letter in the Part II Style Guide chapters

Squint at your Proportion Pattern. Do your shoulders and thighs appear to be about the same width? Is your waist very indented? Does your rib cage taper noticeably inward to your waist and your hips taper noticeably outward from your waist? Mark the shoulder, waist and thigh dots on your Pattern and connect them. If your diagram shapes up like this one, your primary Body Type is **X:** hourglass. But if it doesn't correspond, compare it with the other dot diagrams and see which of the three it most closely resembles. (If you're not **X,** try **A** next; then **H, V.**)

If **X** is your Body Type, look for that letter in the Part II Style Guide chapters

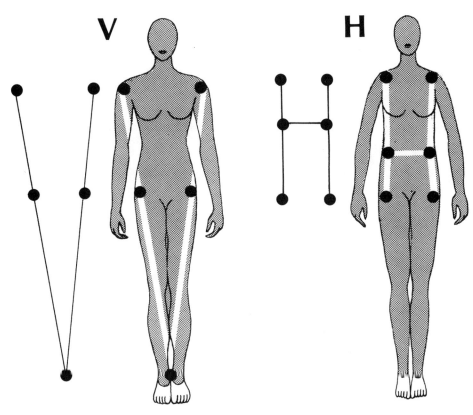

Squint at your Proportion Pattern. Are your shoulders obviously wider than your thighs? Do your hips taper very slightly outward from your waist? Mark the shoulder and thigh dots on your Pattern and connect them. If your diagram shapes up like this one, your Primary Body Type initial is **V:** broad shoulders, narrow waist. But if it doesn't correspond, compare it with the other dot diagrams and see which of the three it most closely resembles. (If you're not **V,** try **H** next; then **X, A.**)

If **V** is your Body Type, look for that letter in the Part II Style Guide chapters

Squint at your Proportion Pattern. Does your rib cage seem to taper in very little toward your waist and do your hips taper only slightly outward from your waist? Is your waist not obviously indented? Do your thighs look only minimally wider than your shoulders? Does your Proportion Pattern silhouette show only slight curves? Mark the shoulders, waist and thigh dots on your Pattern and connect them. If your diagram shapes up like this one, your primary Body Type is **H:** wide-waisted. But if it doesn't correspond, compare it with the other dot diagrams and see which of the three it most closely resembles. (If you're not **H,** try **V** next; then **X, A.**)

If **H** is your Body Type, look for that letter in the Part II Style Guide chapters

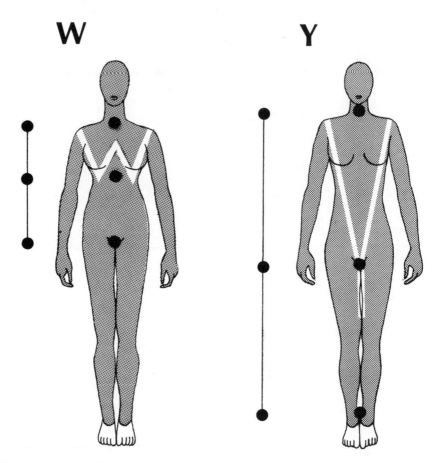

W

Y

Squint at your Proportion Pattern. Does the distance from your shoulders to your waist look about the same as—or less than—the distance from your waist to the point where your legs meet your torso? Mark the neck, waist and crotch dots on your Pattern and connect them. If the line from neck dot to waist dot is the same length or shorter than the line from waist dot to crotch dot, your secondary Body Type initial is **W**: short-waisted. You may also be **Y**, so go on to the **Y** notes.

If **W** is your secondary Body Type, look for that letter in the Part II Style Guide chapters

Squint at your Proportion Pattern. Do your legs appear to be about equally as long as—or only minimally longer than—your torso? Mark the shoulder, crotch and heel dots on your Pattern and connect them. If the line from crotch dot to heel dot is less than 3½ inches longer than the line from crotch dot to shoulder dot, your secondary Body Type is **Y**: short legs, long torso. *Only* if your primary Body Type initial is **H** or **V**, do Step Three. If your primary Body Type initial is **A** or **X**, go on to Step Four.

If **Y** is your secondary Body Type, look for that letter in the Part II Style Guide chapters

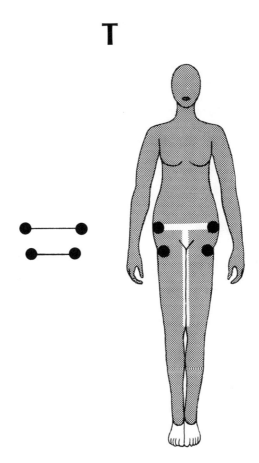

Squint at your Proportion Pattern. Are you noticeably narrower across the tops of your thighs than across your hips? Mark the hip and thigh dots on your Pattern and connect them. If the line across your hips is even slightly longer than the line across the tops of your thighs, add **T:** heavy torso, thin legs, to your Body Type monogram. Now go on to Step Four.

If **T** is one of your Body Type initials, look for
that letter in the Part II Style Guide chapters

STEP FOUR: Profile Body Type Initials

Since your body is not two-dimensional, your proportions seen from the side and from the back affect your image almost as much as how you look head on. Once you've compared your Pattern profile with the four Body Type profile initials here, your proportion survey is complete. All the information you need to use my Style Guide and develop your individual Dress Thin strategy is summed up in the initials of your Body Type monogram. You may be any two- or three-letter combination of profile Body Type initials, but you *cannot* be both an **i** and an **r.** To determine your own profile Body Type initials, visually compare the curves on your profile Pattern with those of the four initials shown, as follows.

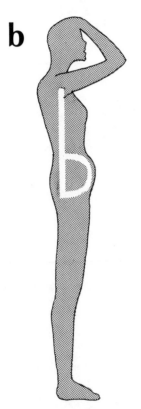

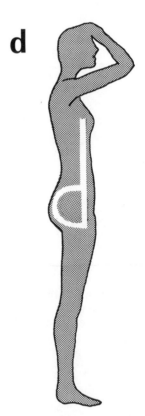

Squint at your Pattern profile. Does your tummy curve outward visibly like the **b** initial shown? If so, add **b,** prominent tummy, to your Body Type monogram.

If **b** is one of your profile Body Type initials, look for that letter in the Part II Style Guide chapters

Squint at your Pattern profile. Does your derrière show a pronounced curve like the **d** initial shown? If so, add **d,** prominent derriére, to your Body Type monogram.

If **d** is one of your profile Body Type initials, look for that letter in the Part II Style Guide chapters

i / r

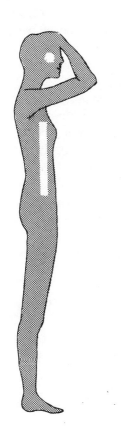 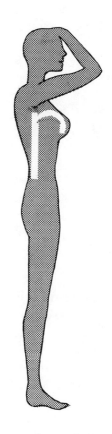

Squint at your Pattern profile. Is your bust curve minimal, like the **i** initial shown? If so, add **i,** small bust, to your Body Type monogram. Or, is your bust curve prominent like the **r** initial shown? If so, add **r,** prominent bust, to your Body Type monogram.

If **i** is one of your profile Body Type initials, look for that letter in the Part II Style Guide chapters

If **r** is one of your Body Type initials, look for that letter in the Part II Style Guide chapters

Write in your Body Type monogram here _____.

Using Control Points to focus on your figure assets

"Control Points" are simply the trimmest and/or most attractive parts of your body: a small waist, slim legs, nice cleavage, neat ankles. Most women use so much energy concentrating on what's amiss, there's none left over for the plus side. Yet your figure assets are the secrets of success, because you can use them to *control* the viewer's eye— to draw it *to* the areas you want noticed, so as to convey an overall positive, thin impression.

By using a small waist as a Control Point, for example, you can draw attention away from heavy hips, derrière, thighs. As you learn my Dress Thin System, you'll see how easy it is to use clothes to underscore your Control Points and put your assets up front. Chapter 10 is the *ultimate* lesson in Control Point strategy.

If you're an **A** Body Type, let's say, you'll find out how to use snugly fitted waistlines and belts to focus the eye on your Control Point waistline. If you're an **r,** you'll find out how you can actually use a neckline that reveals a soupçon of cleavage and just seems to cancel out any impression of top-heaviness. Control Points are a fascinating, simple way to fine-tune your personal Dress Thin technique.

Impact dressing with Dress Thin/Fashion Trade-offs

Once you start using the Dress Thin System to help you shop—in stores or in the fashion pages of magazines—you'll often see exciting clothes you *know* are not Dress Thin potential for your figure type. But let's face it, it's hard to resist the temptation of the latest look. Must you just sigh and turn away as you do (usually) from a 500-calorie slice of chocolate cake?

Interestingly enough, you needn't necessarily deny yourself the fun and impact of fashion for the sake of a thin illusion. The secret is another technique that I call the Dress Thin/Fashion Trade-off. This means you lose *some* but not all Dress Thin value while you gain fashion impact and reinforce your overall image—which of course is the goal of the Dress Thin System. Once again, let's use the **A** Body Type to see how this works.

To Dress Thin, an **A** should correct her proportions with emphasis above the waist, in order to balance heaviness below. She knows she should *not* choose a skirt that adds fullness at the hips. But suddenly one day, dirndl skirts arrive on the fashion scene; they look fresh and new and she can't bear to pass up the look.

What to do?

To start with, choose a controlled dirndl* in a dark or cool[†] color and a soft, drapey fabric. Next, add the all-important jacket that brings the eye up and balances the dirndl's hippiness so you can enjoy the impact of the new fashion. To do its job, the jacket must (1) have padded shoulders or gathers at the

---

*See illustrated definition on page 138.

†See Chapters 3 and 4 for an explanation of how warm and cool colors affect proportion.

shoulders; (2) be the same color as the dirndl or a lighter shade of the same color; (3) be body-skimming, not tight-fitting, and (4) end at or above your hipbone, *never* below.

All these requirements are important, but the shoulder emphasis is the key proportion-correcting element that focuses the eye up and balances the dirndl's fullness. In this example, the jacket clinches the trade-off.

Impact dressing is a Dress Thin technique I first understood by watching the celebrities whose images we see all the time. Very few (if any) of them have perfect figures, yet *some* always look terrific and memorable. They manage this by letting their figures and their personalities interact to create their special fashion impact.

Later we'll talk to some of them and analyze their impact dressing techniques to help you develop your own. Then you can blend those impact techniques into your personal Dress Thin system to ensure that you'll never dress "dull," always dress "up" your own morale—and that of everyone else around you.

Thin is a good fit: What's my size?

From sizes 4 to 44, everybody has one size problem in common: if you go through your closet, chances are that no matter what number you think of as your size, you'll find that it's not the only size you own. I'm sure you've also had the frustrating experience of taking a dress or a pair of pants marked with "your" size to the fitting room, only to discover that it isn't your size at all. And not because you've dieted or haven't dieted or anything radical like that. *You* haven't changed since you bought your last pair of pants, but your size has. So, like the rest of us, you end up with a smorgasbord of sizes in your closet.

It's a confusing situation, and one that often adds to the time consumed in shopping. Unfortunately, however, inconsistent sizing isn't likely to be resolved in the foreseeable future. Because, although the government has established what measurements each size should represent, clothing manufacturers have a variety of reasons for modifying the government-generated basic standards.

Among those reasons, an important one is that designers and their pattern-makers all have their own fit "philosophies" about how clothes should be cut to hug the body in one place or skim it in another. Some of their philosophies may suit the way you are built. Others won't. Size idiosyncrasies can also occur if a designer sees all women in her own body's image. If she has no derrière, for instance, then neither will her clothes—which of course won't fit a woman who does. In still other cases, samples may be fitted on a model whose proportions just don't find echoes in your own.

Finally, there are such factors as manufacturers' economic considerations (some do cut skimpy sizes to save money) and customer-psychology motives ("If she thinks she wears a smaller size in our clothes than in theirs, she'll buy ours . . . !")

Clearly, since sizing confusion is not apt to be straightened out soon, the answer is to stop being intimidated by a number on a tag. Instead, I'll show you two System-atic steps to set you up for terrific Dress Thin fit, and we'll just let the numbers come up as they may.

Take a minute and look in your clothes closet. . . . The fact is that you *should* own more than one size per category of clothing. It's highly unlikely that the same size skirt, for instance, will *always* fit—unless you always wear exactly the same cut, and not many women are *that* conservative. So if you always buy the same size skirt, regardless of cut, you are either incredibly lucky and a veteran lottery winner, or some of your skirts just cannot be helping you Dress Thin. Clothes that don't fit inevitably call attention to exactly the parts of you that you would rather *de*emphasize.

Here are three basic tactics that will help you reduce shopping frustration *and* dress thinner with good-fitting clothes from now on:

1. When you start by choosing a Dress Thin style, you're starting with a fashion idea that makes *visual* sense for your figure. That way, if the garment's *measurements* are off, you still have a fighting chance to achieve a good Dress Thin fit and look. So, when you shop for *anything* to wear, begin by referring to the Style Guide chapters in this book. They give the proportion-correcting style recommendations that are right for you. (Coming up next right here are my Dress Thin Fit Checkpoints, plus suggestions about when to alter what—and when to choose a different style.)

2. When you've located a Dress Thin style, take *two* sizes with you into the fitting room. Just think of the number on each tag as a point of departure— nothing more.

3. Never lose sight of the fact that if a piece of clothing is too small for you, *you* will look *bigger*. Clothes that are slightly loose are basic to your Dress Thin success.

When to alter . . . and when to forget it

When fashion trends change, there's a good chance that there's a new proportion-correcting silhouette in it for you—but sometimes minor alterations can turn your well-chosen purchase into real perfection. In the past, you may or may not have been fully aware of fit problems and their potentially fattening effects. Having done your Body Type I.D. survey, however, you now have the information you need to use fashion changes to your best Dress Thin advantage. Knowing your Body Type, you know which initials are yours. In the section you're reading now, these letters will alert you to particular fit pitfalls for your Body Type, and, in each case, whether to undertake alterations. You'll be surprised at how easily this checklist solves fit and alteration mysteries. (Coming up on page 22, an extensive list of additional Shop Thin hints to save you lots more time and money when you choose new clothes.)

Before checking the Fit Checkpoints, note the following five fundamentals:

1. To make good fit and alteration decisions, you should be wearing whatever underwear you expect to wear with the clothing you're trying on.

2. Sometimes you can even tell with your eyes shut if you have a fit problem—if it *feels* tight anywhere, it won't help you Dress Thin. Look for the problem and correct it.

3. *Any* horizontal pulling or stress lines or wrinkles add pounds—definitely not Dress Thin material.

4. Sleeves that are too short are another giveaway—they should cover your wrists when your arms hang relaxed at your sides.

5. When something's too tight, in most cases I'll recommend buying a size bigger and taking it in. (This is preferable to trying to let out the style because today's seam allowances usually aren't generous enough to give the room you need.)

Checkpoints: Vr

If you are either of the broad-on-top Body Types (whether in the shoulders—**V**—or the bust—**r**), be superalert to all the points listed just below: the neck/shoulders area is crucial to the fit of coats, dresses, jackets and tops of all sorts. If fit is wrong here, it won't be right anywhere.

1. Do you notice any gaping at the neckline?

2. Are there horizontal stress lines stretching all the way across the shoulders of your blouses, dresses, jackets and coats?

3. Watch for pulling at the sides of the garment, just above the bust and across the fullest part of it—front *and* back. If you spot *any* of the hitches mentioned so far, try the next size up. When it fits smoothly without bagging, then have any extra fabric in the midriff taken in. This is a better solution than trying to let out too-tight areas.

4. Wrinkling at the base of the neck means the neckline's too small. It's easy to have a simple jewel neckline loosened; otherwise, choose again.

5. If there are puckers across the upper-arm part of your blouse or dress sleeves, they're too tight. This would be a complicated alteration—you'll do better with a different style.

Checkpoints: H, T, b

Full-through-the-middle Body Types **b, H** and **T** are likely to feel the squeeze in the waistline of pants and skirts, as well as dresses and coats. Even if you can close the garment, *never* buy it if it feels tight—it will also look tight, which is no way to Dress Thin. Instead, buy one size up and take in any excess material in hips and/or thighs. If your dress choice feels too tight in the waist and moving the button *no more than half an inch* will solve it, go ahead. Otherwise, the next size up should fit. (If not, the style's wrong, so pick another.)

Checkpoints: X, W

If you're a curvy **X** Body Type, you may often find that pants and skirts that fit you in the hips/thighs area are too big in the waist. It's more practical to have the waist taken in, rather than to look for pants or a skirt with a waist that fits and try to alter the hips and/or thighs. What's more, for your Body Type, the waist is crucial: The smaller it appears—the bigger you look above and below it. So to equalize your proportions, never wear your skirt or pants waistline tight, or even snug!

If you're the short-waisted **W** type, dresses with waistlines may have too much fabric in the bodice. Rather than try to take in blousiness from the sides—a common mistake—reduce the length of the bodice just above the waist.

Checkpoints: b

Profile **b** Body Types with tummies may see fabric pulling across skirts or dresses below the waist, and hems riding up in front. In any such case, the skirt is not right for your proportions. Choose another style rather than try to alter this one.

Checkpoints: A, X, H, T

If you're a Body Type whose proportions change abruptly from waist to hips—**A, X,** or if your waist is broad—**H** and **T,** you may notice horizontal wrinkles or folds below the waist in the back of pants or skirts. Eliminating them involves having the waistband opened and is a simple alteration that's worth the trouble.

Checkpoints: d

If you're the **d** Body Type, your derrière "padding" may cause stress lines that call attention to the problem. If so, the style was not designed for your proportions; pick one that doesn't pull.

Checkpoints: A, X, T, b, d

Body Types who are heavy anywhere below the waist—**A, b, d, X** and **T**—should be alert for smile lines that radiate from the crotch in pants, and sometimes skirts, as well. To refit pants or jeans with this problem is usually too much of a project—choose a style that doesn't smile. However, if you like a skirt style except that it smiles, you can buy the next size that fits smoothly in the thighs and have the hips and waist taken in.

And that's all there is to recognizing and correcting fit problems that would otherwise undermine your Dress Thin strategy.

Project a thin image: sitting, standing and walking

The Dress Thin System is based on the idea that you can look thinner just by using your clothes to redesign your proportions. In my Dress Thin Style Guide in Part II I'll show you *more than 500 ways* to do that. But right now, learn the *one* Body/Style principle that you can apply immediately to double the effectiveness of all my Dress Thin recipes.

A ballerina phrases it this way:

"Head over shoulders, shoulders over pelvis, pelvis over feet."
—Rebecca Wright, Ballerina,
American Ballet Theatre

A physical therapist says:

"Chin in, stomach in—and the rest of you will fall into alignment."
—Marilyn Moffat, Ph.D., R.P.T.,
Associate Professor of Physical Therapy,
New York University

And for a graphic explanation of *why* good alignment improves your image, listen to an orthopedist whose patients include many ballet dancers:

"If you compress a frankfurter, you'll get a knockwurst! The same amount of stuffing in a smaller space is bound to appear fatter."
—William Hamilton, M.D.
St. Luke's-Roosevelt Medical Center, New York

Every time you slump when you stand, sit or walk, you create that shortened knockwurst effect, and cause your clothes to form wrinkles around the heaviest part(s) of you. Look at a tummy or derrière that sticks out and see how wrinkles, light areas and shadows exaggerate the prominent part, making it look bigger still. If that tummy or derrière happens to be your own, don't be discouraged. "Posture is habitual," says Dr. Hamilton, which means if you pay attention, you can make a habit of *good* posture.

To raise your consciousness and help you realign your body correctly, Dr. Moffat gives these easy-to-follow pointers:

Sitting
Be sure the small of your back is against the back of your chair; draw the chair in close to your desk when you work. Keep chin in when you *sit,* as well as when you stand.

Standing
With your chin and stomach tucked in, imagine pressing the top of your head against the ceiling. Look in the mirror and watch good posture take effect. To experience what proper alignment feels like, stand with your back to a smooth wall, knees slightly bent, and try to flatten your spine against the wall—all the way to the nape of your neck, if possible—that's the hardest part.

19

Walking

Glance at your profile in shop windows as you walk. Are you walking chin first and stomach out? Tuck both in and keep checking to develop and reinforce your good-posture habit. . . .

You're on your way to a Dress Thin image with some backbone to it!

37 Instant Dress Thin how-to's and what-for's

Collected here are the basic tricks and principles that will help you Dress Thin with minimum effort. Some are related to how your clothes fit; others to color, pattern or fabric. Many are just common sense—but we tend to forget or ignore them. Yet as these basics become second nature and you begin to use them routinely, you'll find that each can mean a visual weight loss, plus the morale boost that goes along with it. Enjoy these ways to get *both*, courtesy of clothes, accessories (and a couple of "tools") that you probably already own. . . .

And before you spring for any new clothes, be sure to review my *next* list: 57 Shop Thin ideas to help you make your clothes decisions faster and eliminate purchases that leave your bank account—as well as your proportions—out of balance.

1. Dress Thin in comfortable clothes. Discomfort produces heavy-looking movements.

2. Clothes that pull and show stress lines where you're heavy call attention to those problem areas. If a garment can't be altered to fit properly, out with it!

3. "A little looser is always better."—Pauline Trigère. (She didn't mean baggy, though.)

4. Instead of a girdle, use my Dress Thin System and Style Guide to correct your proportions with *clothes*.

5. If anything you own has tight elastic that produces bulges, banish it. Panty line is a prime culprit . . . turn any panties that are too tight into dustcloths.

6. Slumping adds pounds! Practice *chin in, stomach in* to improve posture and look sleek.

7. Heels that are too high—over 2½ inches—are bad for posture. They force you to push your stomach out for balance. If you must wear them on some occasions, keep a standby pair of low heels handy and switch over whenever possible.

8. Keep your problem areas covered—e.g., if your thighs are heavy, don't wear short-shorts; if your derrière's generous, make sure your swimsuit covers cheeks adequately. (Get a new suit if necessary.)

9. Don't wear a shoulder-strap bag at a length that makes the bag bounce on any heavy area of your body (hips or rear, for instance).

10. Expose and *emphasize* figure assets—good legs with a short skirt, for example.

20

11. If you're heavy, wear good jewelry near your face (earrings, a pin high on the shoulder) to carry the eye upward. Don't just save these precious Dress Thin accessories for special occasions.

12. Tuck your blouses, shirts or tee shirts smoothly into your panties so they won't bunch up and pad your tummy. If pocket linings show through, have them removed and the pockets sewn closed.

13. Breast-droop makes you look heavy—put on a bra that lifts you and watch the pounds come off.

14. Wash your good bra soon after wearing to preserve its support qualities.

15. No matter how small-breasted you are, wear a running or sports bra for active sports. Otherwise, breast-droop *will* result, and soon!

16. *Never* get dressed without consulting a full-length mirror. (If you don't already own one, buy one *today*.) Use a hand mirror to check profile and rear view.

17. Wherever you're heavy, camouflage with dark or cool colors. Stick with very small patterns. (*Cool colors:* blue, green, blue-green, blue-violet, bluish-brown, greenish-brown, bluish or greenish beige and gray.)

18. Wear shoes, hosiery, skirt all in the same color: subtract ten pounds below the waist.

19. Wherever you're thin, spotlight with light, bright or warm colors, something that glitters, or a big pattern element. (*Warm colors:* red, orange, yellow, reddish-purple, red-brown, yellow-brown, reddish or yellowish beige and gray.)

20. Don't wear heavy fabrics that "stand up by themselves," or bulky knits. Dress Thin in supple, thin fabrics, flat knits—and the flatter furs, such as Alaska seal.

21. Cultivate the vertical: sell your horizontally worked fur (or quilted) coat. A vertically worked style will make you look twice as thin. Wear long scarves, vertically striped clothes, dresses that button from hem to neckline (leave top and bottom buttons unbuttoned.) And turn up your collar—especially if you're heavy below the waist.

22. Wear V-necklines. Never button *anything* all the way up. A glimpse of skin carries the eye up and down.

23. When you wear boots, be sure your skirt covers your boot top. A gap between boot and hem is fattening because it interrupts the long body line.

24. Suppress the horizontal: not *just* stripes, also flounces, borders, boat necklines, even ankle-strap shoes and ankle bracelets.

25. Don't wear ruffles anywhere where you're heavy.

26. Skirts and pants that cling reveal too-curvy curves and bulges. An ounce of prevention is worth a lot of pounds, so wear noncling slip under skirts, and panty hose marked ultra-sheer under pants. Also keep a can of antistatic spray handy for emergencies.

27. If you're a jogger, choose running clothes in synthetic fabrics that allow sweat to evaporate so your shorts and tee shirt won't cling to your curves revealingly.

28. *Whatever* proportion problem concerns you, you can minimize it, camouflage it or balance it with a well-chosen suit jacket.

29. If you're not sure whether pants are flattering . . . don't wear them.

30. If you're heavy below the waist, and you own a cape—it's great camouflage—Dress Thin in it.

31. If you're heavy below the waist, wear shoulder pads for balanced proportions.

32. A wrap skirt is great camouflage for tummy, hips and derrière; a wrap dress reduces full bust and waist; ditto for a wrap coat. Subtract five to ten pounds with any of the above.

33. Tummy bulge? Put on a sweater set and watch it disappear.

34. Never wear a belt so tight it makes you bulge above or below it; the best belt is a contour style. Disown anything with a tight elastic waistband. Don't wear a belt on a fur coat (except as a scarf!).

35. If you're short-legged, you can easily look heavier than you are. Don't wear contrast-color belts, or knee socks; have cuffs removed from pants. Wear high heels with pants. Wear dresses and skirts no longer than just below the knee.

36. Everyone's legs look longer and thinner in slingback and backless mule shoe styles.

37. Five pounds off in twenty seconds? Control top panty hose will do it.

57 Shop Thin time and money savers

If you use my Dress Thin System, you'll soon banish costly fashion mistakes forever. Your awareness of your Body Type and the styles that complement it will quickly take hold, and you'll find yourself able to evaluate many things right on the hanger. Shopping is much faster when you know what to look for! You'll astonish—and possibly irritate—saleswomen with your decisiveness as you reject superfluous styling details that add pounds.

Some persistence may be needed to search out the right looks for your proportions—the patch pockets of this world are legion, believe me—but I promise that a successful search will be its own reward. Even at today's prices, your choices will earn their keep because you'll enjoy wearing them for *years*.

This list is full of warnings about items you can leave on the counter without even considering. (Great Dress *Thin*surance against mistakes, because what you leave on the counter will never go on your back—or your bill!) But it also includes some positive suggestions to help you sort through the rows of merchandise and come up with your likely candidates in record time. And once you've read the chapters that follow, the reasons for everything here will be so clear that remembering won't be a problem.

Happy Dress Thin shopping. . . .

1. Use the three-way mirror all three ways: check for bulges in profile and rear view.

2. Close your eyes and check whether anything *feels* tight anywhere. If the answer is yes, don't buy it.

3. Use the Squint Trick to check that your purchase helps create a long bodyline, unbroken by horizontals.

4. Leave the fitting room and find a mirror in which you can see yourself *from a distance.* Repeat the Squint Trick.

5. Experiment with various style combinations in the fitting room. Time spent this way eliminates more time-consuming trips to return things that don't work.

6. Read fabric content tags: consider whether washing will cause shrinkage and play havoc with your careful Dress Thin selection. This applies especially to jeans and tee shirts.

7. Try to take with you on shopping trips whatever shoes and underwear you plan to wear with your purchase(s).

8. If it's on sale, make sure it's also compatible with your Body Type. Otherwise it's no bargain.

9. Think twice (at least) before buying any kind of hairy or pile fabric . . . terry, velour, poodlecloth, mohair, etc., will add five pounds or more, depending on how deep the pile or how long the hair.

10. If you're heavy anywhere below the waist or busty, reject anything with dolman or raglan sleeves—they echo heaviness and make you look dumpy.

11. If you're busty, reject Empire lines and ruffles. Both are maximizing.

12. Unless your legs are flawless, don't wear your hemlines above the knee.

13. Be aware that letting hems down may not always be an option—the original press line may be permanent.

14. If you have a tummy, avoid belted styles.

15. Next time you decide to buy a bra, ask a good fitter for her advice. Bring a sweater and try on all bra possibilities under it.

16. Beige lingerie is a money saver—it works under any color. White shows through many colors, including white.

17. Don't buy a swimsuit with contrast-color trim on any part of you where you're heavy.

18. No matter what your problem area, don't buy a swimsuit with horizontal stripes. If your bust is small, don't buy one with vertical stripes.

19. If you have a tummy, buy a suit with Lycra* in the fabric—it'll hold you in.

20. When buying shoes or accessories, locate a full-length mirror and get the total picture.

---

*Du Pont registered trademark.

21. Warning: Shoes with very thin heels or pointy toes and very delicate sandals exaggerate heaviness in the legs and in the torso above.

22. Don't let a shoe salesperson talk you into the wrong shoe size. Shoes that fit badly contribute to bad posture, which adds pounds.

23. If your torso is heavy, don't buy shoes with heels lower than one inch. They make you look dumpy.

24. Don't buy tight knee-high boots that choke your legs and cause bulges. If the lining is made of leather, you can have boots stretched. Otherwise, buy a different style.

25. Buy "sheer to waist" panty hose to wear under short or slit skirts; other constructions have reinforcement lines that show and make your thighs look heavy.

26. If your legs are heavy, reject semisheer panty hose labeled opaque, and all heavy patterns and textures.

27. If you're heavy anywhere in the torso, don't buy knee socks or anklets. They cut the bodyline and add pounds.

28. Here's how to recognize the instant-thin dress silhouette for you right on the hanger. If you're narrow above the waist but heavy below—choose a dress with fitted bodice and controlled-fullness skirt. If you're narrow below the waist but heavy above—choose a dress with a straight skirt and a full bodice. If you're curvy both above and below the waist, choose a straight chemise silhouette. If your torso is heavy, choose a full caftan silhouette.

29. If you buy a belted dress, one with hidden elastic under the belt is better than one with a seam. Since the elastic gives, it won't cut into your waist and cause bulges.

30. When you buy a suit, try to do it in a store that employs a tailor—or locate your own tailor and treat him or her with kid gloves.

31. Try on double-breasted suits first if you're torso heavy—double-breasted buttons break up torso width.

32. Any suit jacket should have shoulder padding—it's essential to good proportion. If you're straight-up-and-down or heavy below the waist, slightly exaggerated shoulders are a proportion-correcting plus.

33. If you're heavy below the waist, choose squared-off styling rather than a curved jacket hemline that repeats and emphasizes your own curves.

34. A hipbone-length jacket is more flattering to most Body Types than a longer one—it makes your legs look longer.

35. If your jacket has back vents, make sure they don't gape. If they do, buy a different jacket.

36. Ditto if your skirt has inverted pleats.

37. Broad coat or jacket lapels are unflattering to most Body Types. If you're broad-shouldered or busty, choose narrow lapels. If you're small on top—medium to narrow ones are best.

38. If you're shortwaisted, busty, hippy or have a tummy, reject patch and flap pockets; look for inconspicuous pocket styling.

39. Heavy thighs? Get those running or tennis shorts long enough to cover the bulge.

40. Prominent tummy or rear? Avoid waist-length ski parkas and warm-up jackets.

41. Wide waist, or derrière bulge? Buy active sportswear with *tailored* waistbands, not elastic, gathered or drawstring waists.

42. If you have a tummy, avoid open-pleated skirts.

43. Avoid cuffs, patches and tricky seams on jeans and pants if your legs are short.

44. Don't be seduced by tight jeans that seem to slim you in the fitting room. Over the course of the day, body heat produces horizontal stress lines that clearly signal where the proportion problems lie.

45. Never buy a coat that weighs you down—it will make you look as heavy as you feel.

46. If you plan to wear a suit under your coat, wear the suit when you *shop* for the coat.

47. Don't buy a fitted raincoat in a shiny fabric—the highlights will highlight your proportion problems.

48. Don't buy a thick, heavy sweater coat with cables.

49. Buy a coat in a flat fabric. Avoid high-calorie Harris tweeds, plaids, blanket stripes or any horizontal stripes, and curly, hairy or double-faced fabrics. Also reject fur or fake-fur coat *linings*.

50. Fur jackets are fattening unless you have long legs.

51. When in doubt about the length of a fur coat, buy it on the long side.

52. If you're buying a fluffy fur, choose an unbelted style.

53. Don't buy a coat with a lining made of wool or other textured material. It will cling and distort the line of the coat in a fattening way.

54. If you're buying a quilted coat, realize that the thickest insulation isn't necessarily the warmest. Recent synthetic insulators are just as warm as down—and less bulky.

55. It's easier to Dress Thin for a formal occasion than for any other— choose a long formal look, not a short one, in a floaty fabric.

56. If your torso or bone structure is heavy, don't buy tiny jewelry, bags or scarves. Choose oversize sunglasses rather than small ones.

57. Before you shop, read and take notes from the relevant chapters of this book—or better yet, take the book with you!

Dress Thin your own Body/Style

How many times have you read a fashion story and been exhorted to find your "own style"? At least once a month, I'll bet (and I'm a conservative bettor). But how often has the writer told you *how* to find it? Well, this time you will get something tangible to go on—as tangible as your own figure. By now, I don't think you'll be surprised to hear me say that there is no better starting point.

Here's an extreme analogy to illustrate why this is true. Suppose you regard strawberry shortcake as absolutely the most beautiful taste sensation you could ever wrap your tongue around . . . but whenever you follow that inclination, you get hives from head to foot. Strawberry shortcake therefore suits your taste ideally—but is a great mistake for your body. Regretfully but intelligently, you swear off strawberry shortcake.

In interviewing ten vastly attractive women each of whose image must be carefully cared for because of her constant contact with one kind of audience or another, I found every one an expert on which clothes her figure is "allergic" to, and which it thrives on. With this vital body knowledge as a foundation, each then builds into her image the intangibles of personality—while taking into consideration the constraints of her lifestyle, as well. (But as for "following" fashion, you'll note that that's completely *out*.) The end result for each woman is her *individual Body/Style*.

Having analyzed your own Body Type, you're *at least* as aware of your proportions as any of the women I'm about to describe, and the Style Guide chapters will soon show you which clothes do and don't agree with your Body Type. The purpose of the interviews that follow is to demonstrate how to put together Body Type + personality + lifestyle elements in a total Body/Style mix that works. (The idea is to copy the *process*, of course, not the person.) My interview subjects are such expert Dress Thin strategists that unless they verbally pinpointed proportion problems, I could only make educated Body Type guesses as to what they were; that's why there are some question marks among their Body Type initials.

Michelle Savitt Tepper **(Vb)**
Image: Flamboyant. *Occupation:* Co-founder and designer, M & J Savitt fine jewelers

Michelle Savitt's flamboyant image instantly signals that she is an integral part of New York's fashion community. However, fashion is obviously her slave, not the other way around. Individual and exciting as they are, for her, *clothes* are the accessories, her face and jewelry the main event! Your eye is immediately drawn *up* to a sexy red mouth and brown eyes below dark bangs, which, with her very long, thick ponytail, have been her trademark for ten years. Next, you notice the small waist, accented by a wide belt. Thanks to the flowing ballerina-length skirts she favors, plus long necklaces and earrings and the vertical sweep of ponytail—your impression is of a person even taller than her 5 feet 6 inches. Because her business is fashion, she can and does dress as exotically as she pleases (at night when there is more time to be creative, she says her clothes can be even wilder). But the Body/Style she projects is an extension of her vivacious, intense personality. No wonder that the tummy she confides is her proportion problem goes undetected. No surprise, either, when she says that as long as she looks feminine and sexy, she never worries that she might "overdress." To Michelle, "being one of a crowd of look-alikes" is the unpardonable sin—not overdressing.

Paula Hughes **(Ai)**
Image: Understated. *Occupation:* First Vice-President and Director, Thomson McKinnon Securities

Stockbroker Paula Hughes, who admits to being one of the highest paid salespersons in the U.S., says there is no fashion formula for business success. "You will succeed because of what you offer professionally, not because of what you wear—except to the extent that what you wear reinforces and helps you project your confidence," she insists. A classic **A** Body Type, Paula focuses attention on the small waist that she singles out as her best feature. "A full skirt makes it look even smaller," she points out. With two-part dresses in summer and suits in winter, she stresses continuity of color from shoulders to hemline, plus coordinating shoes and hosiery, and avoids "horizontal interruptions that would emphasize my hips." Her shoulder-length hair also contributes to the total effect of verticality. "You don't have to assume masculine traits to achieve," she says, and enjoys projecting femininity, but she needs no ruffles or lace to do it. With unusual choices of jewelry and scarves and a passion for handbags and shoes, she makes a statement but not an overstatement about individuality. Preferring to "decide how to invest a million dollars than face a rackful of dresses," she demonstrates her expertise at what corrects her proportions by successfully shopping by mail! Thus liberated, she's able to spend precious leisure hours at the opera, the ballet or on the tennis court rather than in a store. Paula's understated Body/Style approach serves admirably both to bring her professional competence to center stage and to spotlight her figure assets.

Peggy Lyman **(Vi)**
Image: Confident. *Occupation:* Principal dancer, Martha Graham Company

With her superb dancer's carriage and 5 foot 11 inch stature, Peggy Lyman projects utter confidence. Completely at ease with her broad shoulders and height, she attempts no fashion camouflage, but dresses simply, hair pulled back for a small-head look that reinforces the thinnest-possible illusion. She says her shoulders are a trademark—"Part of who I am—so I would never choose frills or anything that would soften or hide them." This is great Dress Thin strategy for the scale of her body, since if her shoulders were hidden, the *rest* of her would appear big. Correctly, however, she does avoid Empire-line dresses that would visually isolate her shoulders, and very revealing necklines designed for a fuller bustline than hers. She also hopes for costumes that are not too long-waisted so as not to exaggerate an already long torso. In dance classes and on stage, clingy costumes and practice clothes are so revealing that when she's not dancing she enjoys wearing something loose (but never shapeless), "so I can rest my abdomen." For a black tie gala, she walks a fine line between drama and flamboyance. "I don't want a dress that wears me. You should say 'Look at Peggy' not 'Look at that dress.' " Good legs mean she can and does adopt any hemline. She enjoys trying on unfamiliar fashion ideas. "Very often I'll buy something that appeals to me and discover later that it happens to be what the fashion world had in mind for me." Peggy's confident Body/Style expresses itself in her posture and in "clothes I can feel at home in anywhere."

Renée Poussaint **(Ad?)**
Image: Authoritative. *Occupation:* Anchorperson, WJLA-TV Evening News, Washington, D.C.

As a Chicago TV journalist, Renée Poussaint learned to "dress with no idea whether I'd be chasing a fire engine or attending a reception." Now anchoring the news in the nation's capital, she still needs versatile clothes but they must also manage to project both authority and personality *without* distracting the viewing audience. She explains that a woman anchor must avoid substantiating the notion that "news coming from a woman's mouth sounds like gossip." In addition, Renée must wear "color that comes forward but doesn't scream," so that the earth tones of her skin don't blend into Channel 7's beige-and-gray set. Altogether a tall order, but one that 5 foot 7 inch Renée handles adroitly—simultaneously compensating for some below-the-waist heaviness that she says runs in her family. Trained in dance, she has analyzed her figure with a dancer's keen eye. Her Dress Thin techniques emphasize her height: short, Afro'd hair and clothes with simple vertical lines; often, a jacket—but not every night, because "that would convey a false image of me; I'm not a one-dimensional person." So she varies her look with a vertically looped scarf or an open-collared dress or blouse. To distinguish her face from the neutral set, Renée has amassed a novel collection of smallish, bright-colored earrings and pins . . . an inventive tactic that both expresses her strong personality and solves an on-the-job technical problem in one Body/Style coup.

Elke Sommer **(Vr)**
Image: Casual. *Occupation:* Actress

Not every sexy star requires a thick layer of studied glamor to get her message across. Elke Sommer is one who enjoys casual elegance and is an example of the broad-shouldered **V** Body Type that carries off clean-line, breezy clothes so well. Her Dress Thin strategy—including marvelous posture—is so effective that she would feel comfortable wearing her own clothes in front of the camera, even though "the camera adds pounds." It took time and concentration, she admits, to refine her awareness of what flatters the 5 foot 7 inch proportions she describes as "unmatched: size medium on top, petite on the bottom." She's candid about dressing to please her husband by accentuating her small waist with a full skirt, for example, and by complementing her long neck and full bust with open necklines that preclude a top-heavy effect. She never makes the mistake of wearing "anything too tight—tight clothes make even a slim woman look heavy," yet insists on styles that show the shape of her figure. This has been a rule ever since a movie fashion designer put her in a shapeless polka-dot number that made her look "roly-poly." Less is definitely more, she agrees, and, "Overdoing it is easy: add a wrong note and you ruin the whole effect. To make it elegant, underdo it . . . make it simple." Which is just what Elke does, creating an integrated Body/Style image that doesn't proclaim "Star!" because on camera or off, no announcement to that effect is necessary.

Patti Wilson **(Hi)**
Image: Zany. *Occupation:* Freelance photographer's stylist

The more fashion imagination Patti Wilson projects via her own image, the better she advertises her impressive styling ability to prospective clients. She can and does wear anything—*provided* it helps her visually lengthen her 5 foot 3 inch line. Even though she's in the fashion business, she declines to adopt the latest look for its own sake if it doesn't work for her Body Type—when "baggies" were in, she put them on models but *not* on herself. On the other hand, when low heels came back strongly, she chose to limit herself to flat shoes, but still managed to look taller than she is! How? By "letting the long line of my neck show. I pull my hair back and wear no accessories from the bustline up. I adore accessories, so first I pile them on . . . then I *edit*." Necklaces are not for her, but "when I fell in love with a wonderful lariat, I just wore it wrapped around my wrist." (She could also have wrapped it around her waist as a belt, or slung it diagonally from shoulder to waist.) Patti's Body/Style blends the kooky charm of her personality with her professional mastery of Control Point strategy. She practices Dress Thin Fashion Trade-offs like a religion of which she's the high priestess.

Ann Berk (Hi?)

Image: Streamlined. *Occupation:* Station manager, WRC-TV, Washington, D.C.

At just 5 feet 3½ inches tall, Ann Berk's image is still best summed up as streamlined—which dovetails neatly with the demands of her high-powered job and busy life. Predictably, for one who holds the distinction of having been TV's first woman station manager of a network-owned (NBC) station, her aim is: "To do many things well without wasting time on the less important ones, like dressing." Not having the time or patience for a lot of shopping—"I don't like to mix and match, or wear fussy clothes or accessories," she says, "a dress is often my solution; it's a one-process thing. I can get up, put it on and be happy in it . . . get my daughter ready for school, walk the dog and do everything that needs doing before I go to the office at eight or eight-thirty." The narrow-silhouette dresses she prefers, generally in cool or neutral colors, are the perfect Dress Thin choices to give her the uninterrupted streamlined effect she likes. If the dress has a contrast-color belt to mark her small waist, all the better. Slingback shoes plus sheer hosiery in unified tones lengthen and minimize her legs. In winter, especially, she may also use the alternate stream-lining tactic of a straight skirt plus a silk blouse with a little shoulder padding to carry the eye up and create a slimmer illusion below. "I'm not a suit person," she emphasizes, "because I like the kind of narrow, unbulky winter coat that doesn't have room for a jacket underneath—and in the office, I'm always running like crazy, so I'd only take the jacket off." The woman manager's suit-and-attaché-case style cliché is "the opposite of me." Further, "What one 'should' like is not the point," says Ann. "It takes time to find yourself and to learn to recognize clothes that are 'you'; an air of authority comes when you're comfortable with yourself and do your job well. Not from your clothes."

Annette Golden (Ab?)

Image: Dramatic. *Occupation:* Senior Vice-President and General Manager, Revlon "Classic" Division

It's possible that a high-level executive in the cosmetics industry might be mistaken for her counterpart in banking—but not if the executive is Annette Golden. Within the confines of a rigorous schedule that can start with an eight-fifteen breakfast meeting and end at seven or seven-thirty, the woman responsible for the success of Jontue and for Revlon's newest fragrance, Scoundrel, projects an image that's pure drama. To maximize her 5 feet 5 inches, she tends toward a one-color look from shoulders to hem, but achieves it with spare dresses, suits or separates, as the spirit moves her. Tightly woven natural fabrics such as heavy silk are preferred for their ability to stand up to her long day without wilting, and repeated trips to the dry cleaners. Dramatic statements that express what she calls her "eccentricity" are made with dashing hats, eye shadow and scarves; bold jewelry and belts. Long and unusual necklaces are chosen both to lengthen a roundish face and establish a focal point on her trim upper torso. She likes what she wears to have a defined bodice, rejecting anything that's either formless or very clinging below the waist. Bought by the dozen for essential shopping efficiency, her panty hose are control top for that "nice feeling of firmness." Very high heels are tempting but ruled out by her three-mile walk to the office. Does she ever wear pants to work? "Very rarely, since they're not the most flattering possibility for me." But at home or in the country, she relaxes in jeans or pleated pants ("great because they're not fitted in the thighs"). And at night, a black silk jumpsuit or red chiffon tunic and tapered pants communicate the kind of bold Body/Style flair that's characteristically Annette.

Cathy Rigby **(Vi)**
Image: Natural. *Occupation:* Gymnast, sportscaster, actress

Although petite (4 feet 11½ inches)—Cathy Rigby cannot truly be said to have a proportion problem—the sunny ex-Olympic gymnast does have a tendency to gain weight in her thighs. When that happens, she's careful to Dress Thin in loose clothes that don't betray extra pounds. A thinning technique she used as a gymnastics competitor and now recommends to students in gymnastics clinics is the sidestripe that so magically elongates the bodyline of anyone taking part in an active sport. When she's interviewed on camera, her confident, erect athlete's bearing still helps her establish presence, but until recently her height made it difficult to project the grown-up image needed to advance her budding career as an actress and singer. What she wears is crucial in this respect, and she has picked up useful ideas from the stylists who work with her on TV commercials. The first step toward a more mature Body/Style approach was to trade in her blond braids for a short close-to-the-head haircut to capitalize on the taller illusion created by a small head. She's learned to avoid contrasting belts that "cut me right in half" and frills which are out of scale, suggesting "a kid dressing up like Mom." Rather, she now wears simple dresses in silk and other soft fabrics to help her project sex appeal when a role calls for it, and a suit or tailored separates for TV sportscasting. Cathy tries to choose light colors that increase her height and make her look more important, but correctly steers clear of ultra-sophisticated clothes that would clash with the naturalness that is her charm.

Julie Schafler **(Xd?)**
Image: Individualist. *Occupation:* Owner, Julie Artisans Gallery

"When I try on designer clothes, I feel I'm dressing in someone else's personality," says Julie Schafler who blended her Master's degree in art history with her interest in fashion into an innovative business selling art objects that are created to be worn. At the same time, of course, she developed the source of a personal image that both perfectly expresses her aesthetic and offers unique proportion-enhancing possibilities. Even when she isn't wearing an original from her gallery, her costume always includes something made by hand—an ethnic or period piece that retains "a sense of contact with the person who made it, so it's never anonymous or lifeless," she says. This collection forms the nucleus of her wardrobe; to fill in around it, she shops for clothes that complement but don't compete. As a classic small-waisted **X** Body Type, her Dress Thin strategy is to draw the eye to her waist with a one-of-a-kind belt, or else to her upper torso—with an antique shawl, for example, or an elaborate macraméd top. Her lower torso goes unnoticed under a full, calf-length skirt; depending on the season, boots or sling-back sandals complete the picture. The visual excitement at the top of her torso gives the illusion that she's at least two inches taller than her 5'5½". "Luckily, I'm usually attracted to things that suit my Body Type," Julie notes, "but when there's a conflict, it's easy to resolve. I just hang the piece on the wall and admire it there." That capacity to be objective about whether something looks beautiful—and whether it looks beautiful on *her*—is essential to Julie's (and anyone's) Body/Style success.

PART TWO

The Complete Dress Thin System Style Guide

1. Dress Thin in Almost Nothing
Swimwear

Let's be honest: women do dress to be admired. Otherwise, you'd never have opened my book. And what I want you to have by the time you finish it is the basis for a special kind of confidence in how you dress. A confidence that comes only from knowing what you're doing, instead of having to guess, when you put on a piece of clothing. Once you understand my System for changing your proportions with clothes, every time you Dress Thin, you'll bask in admiring glances. Even on the beach.

Yes, even on the beach or by the pool, where, as I'm sure you've noticed, confidence is at a premium, but there's more than enough self-consciousness to go around.

How many women do you know who really look forward to beach season? The minute the fashion pages and the stores fill up with swimwear, most of *us* are filled with pure dread. And before we can say "diet," much less do it, the season is here. A lot of women I know would rather settle for last year's suit than face that fitting room mirror.

Ever since I've been designing swimwear, I've been giving it to my best friends for Christmas. Of course, I choose each suit carefully, with their Body Types in mind. My friends never seem to have heard of "Do not open till Christmas." The minute they put those suits on, the resort travel agents start working overtime and my mail box fills up with glowing postcards.

How come? What's my incredible swimsuit secret? Just this: *the less you wear, the more the System helps.*

That's what this chapter is all about. All you have to do to be as beach-happy as everyone on my Christmas list is—as the magicians like to say—to watch closely. Because once *you* understand my proportion-based Dress Thin System and the illusion techniques that make it work, you, too, can find the bathing suit(s) that let you look thinner even if you never get around to that diet you've been promising yourself. And what if you're too thin somewhere—small-breasted, for instance? You'll find my System can also help you put yourself in better, more flattering proportion.

Using the information in this chapter along with everything I taught you about your particular proportions in Part I, you'll be able to choose your next suit painlessly! No matter whether you're hung up on your hips, touchy about your tummy, depressed about your derrière—or *any* of the other sore spots we agonize over—you'll be equipped to walk into that fitting room without a qualm. And to walk out with a swimsuit choice (or three) for which you'll mentally thank me whenever you stroll onto the beach. (I'm expecting a record wave of postcards in the near future!)

Before I show you how to recognize the swimsuit styles or "cuts" that will work best for you, I'd like to explain the important difference that fabrics can make. Because, especially in swimwear if you choose it knowledgeably, fabric can do as much for your figure as cut. Stretchy or rigid fabric? Smooth or plush texture? Dark-colored or light? Print or solid? My System will guide you to the right answers for your own Body Type.

Swim Thin fabric construction. First, a key point about swimwear fabric construction. Most swimsuits today are made of fabrics that, whether knitted or woven, are stretchy rather than rigid. But there is also a category of suits made of rigid cotton or cotton/synthetic blend fabrics. (When you shop, you can recognize a rigid fabric by pulling with both hands: top to bottom, side to side—it won't stretch either way.)

If you don't exercise at all and your figure is flabby, bathing suits made of these rigid fabrics are worth considering since their rigidity does control and camouflage torso flabbiness in the same way that a woven-fabric dress does. Many swimsuits made of rigid fabrics also minimize the bust because the fabric's rigidity has a flattening effect; or, they may have side bones or cup inserts that support the bust and emphasize it.

In choosing either a rigid or a stretch-fabric suit, check to make sure it's not made with heavy elastic in the legs that will cut into your thighs and cause bulges. You can't Dress Thin in *any* swimsuit that causes thigh bulge!

If you choose a rigid-fabric suit for its camouflage potential, you should also be aware that it will be restrictive and less comfortable than a suit made of stretch fabric that moves with you. Therefore, as a designer, I recommend today's *stretch* swimwear fabrics (usually knitted, sometimes woven) as the better way to control and support your figure in a bathing suit.

When you try on a suit made of one of these elastic stretch fabrics, you'll notice its smoothing, firming effect on your body. In addition, if you're a B cup or smaller, these technologically advanced fabrics actually support your breasts without the use of bones or padding. Depending on styling, stretch fabric suits can even support a firm C bust: look for a one-piece style with a seam under the bust. And in fact, if you're game to play sculptor with your body, a stretch fabric suit will help you.

To fully exploit the fabric's molding and support capabilities, give *it* a little help: after you pull on your stretch maillot, cup a hand under each breast and push it up and forward. Watch what happens in the mirror and experiment until you achieve a nice, lifted look. Your stretch suit will keep your bust right where you want it until you go swimming. (Readjust under water just before emerging!)

A *long-legged illusion* is a big assist for *everybody's* Dress Thin in Almost Nothing strategy. Thanks—again—to stretch fibers, there's an instant longer-legs technique that works *best* with a stretch fabric maillot (the fashion term for a one-piece suit) though you can use it with any one-piece style that has *elastic legs*. My dancer friends taught me this trick, and in turn I've taught it to quite a few models. They love the quick and startling improvement it makes in *their* total proportion picture, and so will you. If you're the short-legged **Y** Body Type, it's indispensable. Basically, all this technique involves is adjusting your swimsuit legs so that more of *your* legs show. The illustrations on page 38 show exactly how to do this.

Whether your suit is two-piece or a maillot, you can manipulate the stretch fabric to give your derrière a lift, too. Keep watching in the mirror (from profile) and see what a difference a little push upward will make if your derrière tends to droop. Stretch fabrics are a lot cheaper than plastic surgery, right?

To recognize a suit with these wonderful talents, look for labels or hangtags that specify Lycra or spandex, both of which are names for the synthetic rubber fibers that impart stretch and recovery. Incidentally, *without* these fibers, your swimsuit will become baggy when it gets wet—definitely not a look for anyone who wants to Dress Thin!

The percentage of stretch fiber in swimsuits does vary: a higher percentage number *may* mean the suit will give more control and support, but the only way to verify this is by trial. So, as you select your Dress Thin styles based on the illustrations in this chapter, note the Lycra or spandex percentage specified on their labels. When you try on the suits, you'll be able to tell immediately which fabrics do the most for you.

Although flat fabrics are the most common in swimwear, fashion trends sometimes bring into the picture heavy textures such as terry cloth, puckered materials or plushy velours. Fabrics like these make you look just a touch heavier where your suit *is*, but thinner where it isn't. This is a real advantage if you're an **A** Body Type who has heavy thighs in proportion to her torso. When you put on a maillot made of one of these thicker-textured fabrics, you'll see that your legs appear thinner, your overall proportion balance improves and you've just found a great way to Dress Thin for the beach.

Proportion-correcting with color value. Many people are aware that dark colors produce a thinner illusion and light ones make the body look heavier. But to use this commonly accepted wisdom in your Dress Thin swimwear strategy, it's helpful to understand *why* it is so.

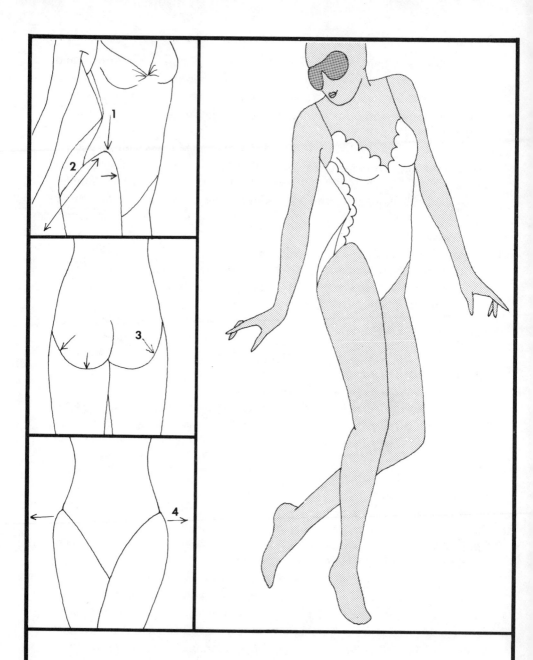

Lengthen your legline to Dress Thin in Almost Nothing

A long-legged, taller illusion is basic Dress Thin swimsuit strategy for all Body Types. To create this illusion, your swimsuit must have elastic legs. **(1)** Pull each up toward your hipbones *in front*; **(2)** keep tops of outer thighs covered; **(3)** pull down over buttocks in back; **(4)** do one leg at a time and *don't* pull straight up at sides, which exposes bulges. At all costs, *avoid* a straight-across legline. If you're under six feet tall, it's guaranteed to make you look dumpy.

The reason that dark-value colors are thinning is that they *absorb* light and create no obvious shadows to outline bumps and bulges. Conversely, light-value colors *reflect* light and do cause shadow outlines wherever anything sticks out. This makes it possible for you to exploit the *contrast* of a dark torso with light shoulders, arms and legs (or the reverse if you're black) to create illusions that *balance* proportions, too.

If you've ever taken a painting class, you may know that artists describe colors as "warm" or "cool." Interestingly, this temperature aspect of color can also help you Dress Thin in Almost Nothing. Here, the point to remember is that (like dark-value colors) cool colors deemphasize because they appear to recede. Thus, choose a suit with cool blue, blue-green or blue-purple bra if you're a busty **r** Body Type, and with one of those colors below the bustline if your proportion problem is tummy **(b)**, derrière **(d)**, thighs **(A, X)** or hips **(A, T, X)**. (For more detailed warm- and cool-color Dress Thin techniques, see Chapters 3 and 4.)

By now you can see that a simple "wear dark—avoid light" bathing suit rule doesn't do justice to all the proportion-correcting illusions that color can create in swimwear. For certain Body Types, suits that are entirely or partly light-colored are actually the *best* choices. If you're a small-breasted **i** type, you can maximize your bust by wearing a dark maillot with a light-colored bra area, or a two-piece style that has a dark bottom and a light bra. If you're an **A** or **X** with heavy thighs, or a **Y** with short legs and you color your torso darker than your skintone, you only exaggerate your proportions instead of balancing them. See how this basic principle works in the illustration on page 40, where I've compared two different Body Types in both dark and light color-value suits.

Dark-value colors and small prints on dark backgrounds are both good swimwear strategies for you if your Body Type is **b, d, r, T, W** or **X.** Don't forget, though, that "dark" includes a whole spectrum of proportion-balancing shades beyond black and navy blue: try deep greens, browns, burgundy and purple tones, too.

For the small-breasted Body Type **i** and the **A** who is small above the waist and heavy below, a contrast swimsuit strategy based on a bra that's light-colored or has a splashy print and a dark, solid torso or bottom, effectively equalizes your proportions. And whatever your Body Type, remember this key rule about color contrast in swimsuits: never buy a suit with a contrast color element on a part of your body you don't want observers to focus on.

There's also lots of proportion-correcting potential in prints for various Body Types, depending on the size and placement of the pattern elements. Key examples of nongeometric prints are shown on page 41, and the chapter illustrations include many swimsuits with geometric design elements that create proportion-correcting illusions you'd never dream of.

Fabric construction, color and texture all play important Dress Thin roles in swimwear, but they're only the beginning.

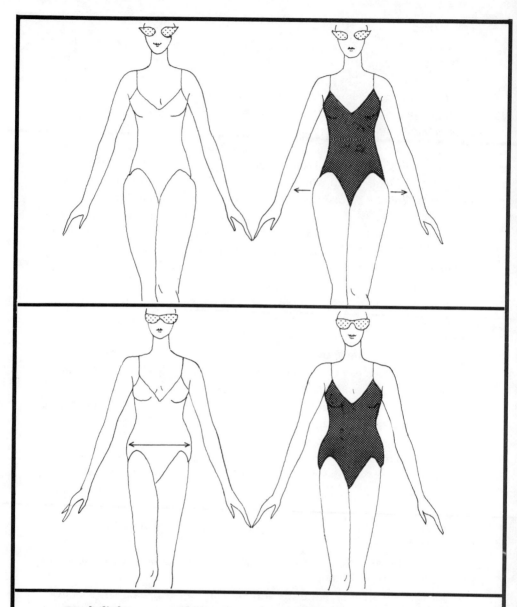

Dark/light proportion-correcting techniques for swimwear

A dark swimsuit makes the **A** Body Type's heavy thighs look heavier, while a suit that approximates the light tone of her skin makes the heaviness less obvious. If you're black, your suit should be a lighter color value than your skin, or the same value, but *not* darker.

For the **T,** a dark-value suit contrasts with the light skintone of her legs to help reverse the bigger/smaller proportional relationship: the contrasting lightness of the legs *reinforces* the minimizing effect of a dark color value on the torso. If you're black, your suit must be *much* darker than your skintone for this illusion to work for you.

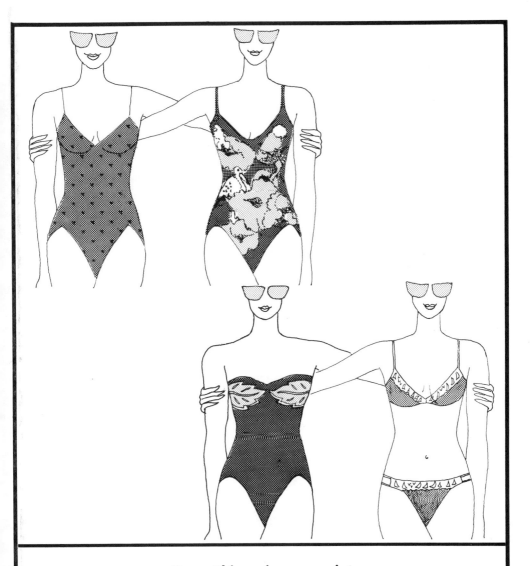

Dress Thin swimwear prints

Allover prints with small designs on dark-value grounds (top left) are good minimizers for both full bust (**r**) and lower-torso heaviness types **A, d** and **X.** Follow my "rule of pinky" to get the right size print: the design should not be bigger than the last joint of your pinky finger. A big print on a dark-value ground plays down curves for the **X** and camouflages the **i** type's small breasts.

You can use a print with just one element (bottom left) to focus on a Control Point and help correct proportion balance. This example would work well to deemphasize hips for **A, T** and **X** Body Types. A border print calls attention to the parts being outlined, so this suit (bottom right) would be a poor choice for heavy-below-the-waist **A, d** and **X,** and for the **b** type's tummy. But it creates emphasis in the right places to help balance the proportions of Body Types **H, V** and **W.**

Using my instructions in Part I, you've already done an objective Proportion Pattern survey of your figure and determined your Body Type initials. In the following pages, I'll show you a range of swimsuit style possibilities for your Body Type and explain how they can change your proportions—which ones will let *you* Dress Thin in Almost Nothing, and which to *avoid* to look your thinnest. When you see any of your Body Signs slashed with a diagonal bar, the illustrations on that page show "don'ts" for you.

Be sure to mark all the illustrations that describe the illusions, camouflage tricks and proportion-balancers I recommend for your particular figure. Then take the book with you when you shop and you'll know just which styles to take into the fitting room and which you don't even have to bother with. Most—if not all—of the ones you do try on will be flattering candidates for your swimwear wardrobe. Instead of wondering whether you'll ever find *one* that you like, you'll wonder how you'll ever find a way to pay for all the swimsuits you *love* on your figure.

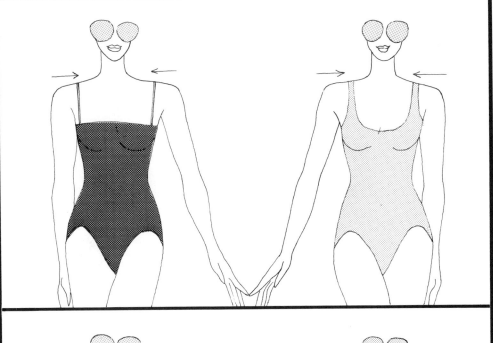

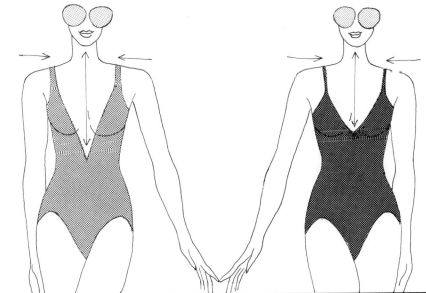

Minimize shoulders

If you have bony shoulders or broad ones (**V**), straps that are slightly set in (above left) "trap" the eye, so your shoulders go unnoticed. Straps of the classic tank suit (right) accomplish the same purpose. The illusion of a longer neck decreases the **V** Body Type's shoulder width—the styles in the bottom row with their deeply plunging necklines do this effectively.

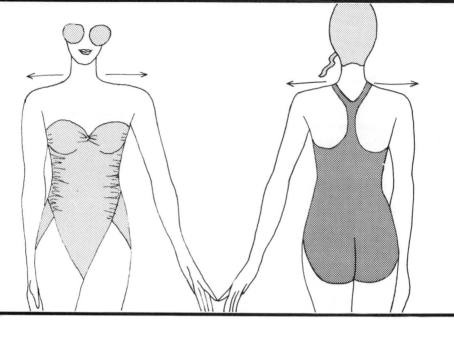

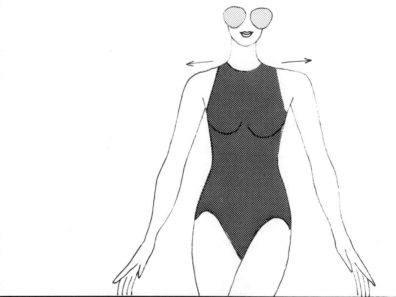

Broad shoulders? Don't . . .
Busty? Cover up . . .

These covered-up suits shorten the neck and broaden the shoulders—not for you if you're the **V** type. Your best bets are all on the previous pages. If you're the busty **r** type, however, a *dark* suit with maximum coverage above the waist, like one of these, is a good Dress Thin choice.

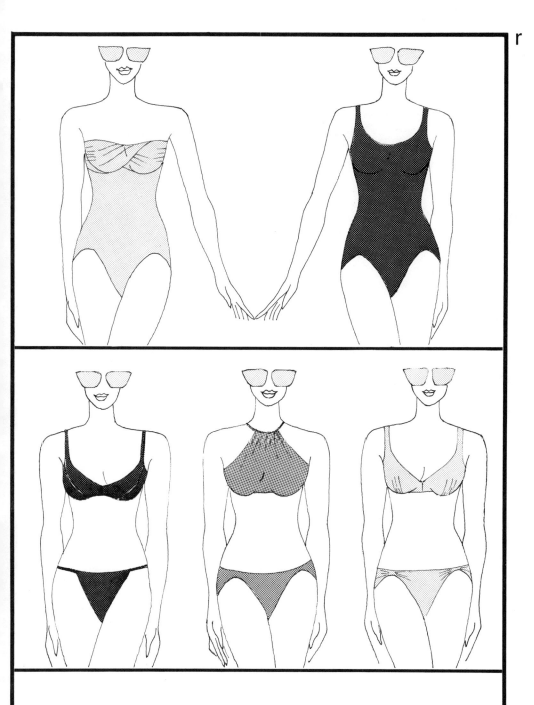

Camouflage full bust

For the **r** Body Type, these flattering high-cut covered-up suits are ideal if you're self-conscious in barer styles because your bust overflows and/or bounces uncomfortably.

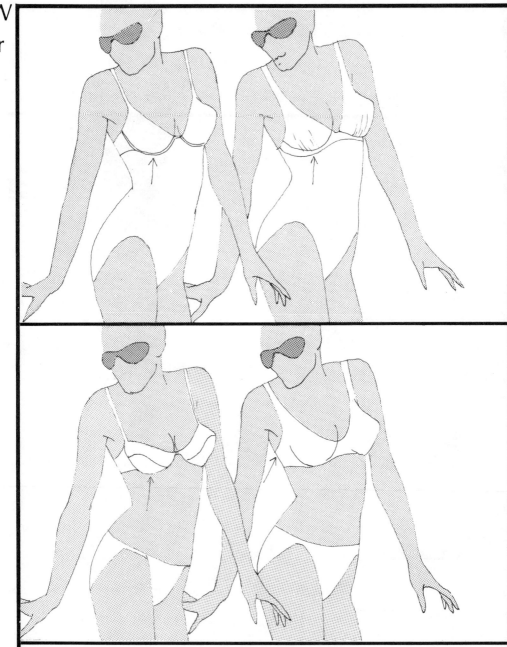

Control full bust,
lengthen short waist

Maillots and bikinis for busty **r** Body Types have supporting underwire bras (top two) and/or wide-set strap styles (below) whose strap width gives support from *sides*. If you're the short-waisted **W** type, the underwire bra suits are good lengthening strategy for you.

Heavy above the waist? Don't . . .
Small on top? Maximize . . .

For the small-breasted **i** Body Type, horizontal-striped or print-bra'd maillots and bikinis like these are maximizing. Also a good option for you is a maillot that's light on top, dark in the torso (top left and right). None of these is good strategy for broad-shouldered **V** or busty **r** Body Types.

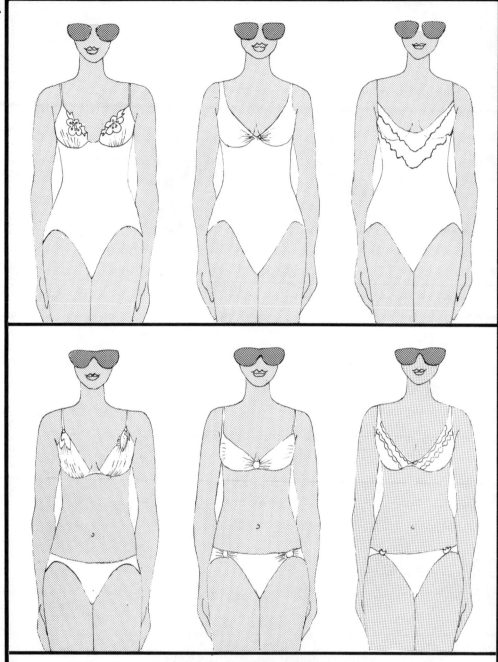

Small on top? Maximize . . .
Full bust? Don't . . .

For small-above-the-waist, heavy-below **A** Body Types and the small-busted **i**, these six suits add what you need—width at the top. For the **A**, gathers and ruffles at the bust help balance weight below the waist.

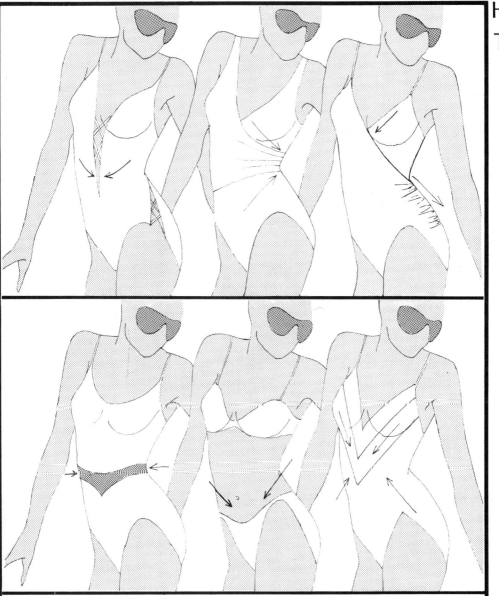

Narrow your waist

Six maillots that narrow your waist if you're an **H** or **T** Body Type. In each case, the arrows show how the suit style narrows your waistline. (You're training your Dress Thin eye!) The straight-up-and-down **H** Body Type can create the illusion of a waist by adding a belt to a maillot. If you're an **H** *with a flat tummy,* you'll appear to have a waistline if you adjust the elastic waist of your bikini so it dips down (bottom row center). The arrows show how the pared-down maillot creates a waist by focusing the eye on the midpoint of your body.

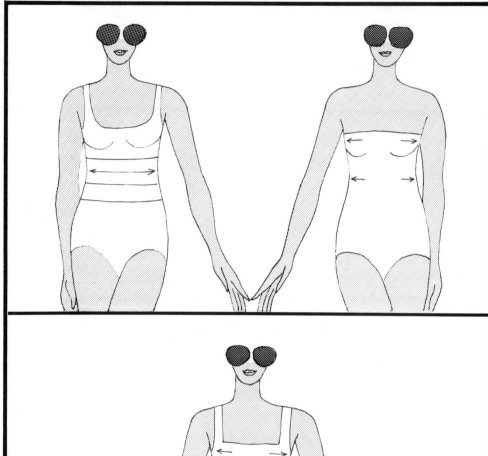

Wide in the middle? Don't . . .
Curvy <u>X</u> type? Balance proportions . . .

If you're a straight-up-and-down **H** type or a torso-heavy **T** body, horizontal lines put you in a waistless box shape! But if you're a very curvy **X** Body Type, you can use styles like these to correct your proportion balance. (Avoid straight-across legs, though—maximum leg length is desirable for all.)

Minimize tummy, lengthen short waist

A pared-down, scooped-out maillot appears to decrease the **b** type's tummy width and lengthen the **W** body's short waist. Dark colors that camouflage help, too. More camouflage tactics for the **b** type's tummy include: the blouson (top center); a suit with a body-skimming skirt (bottom row) that flares slightly (fabric should *not* cling); or, try a maillot with a diagonal design that pulls the eye away from the tummy. And for best tummy control, don't forget to check that the fiber content label in your suit says Lycra or spandex.

b

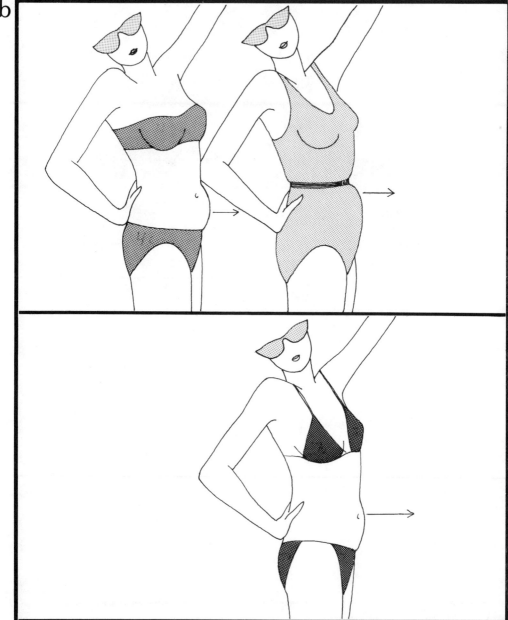

Tummy bulge? Don't . . .

If you're the **b** type, don't get a bikini bottom that cuts across and accentuates bulge; always adjust the elastic of your two-piece swimsuit bottom to place it *below* the point where your tummy curve begins. Never belt your swimsuit, and don't be tempted by string bikinis. (Belts are good tactics for an **H** type with a flat tummy, as described on page 49.)

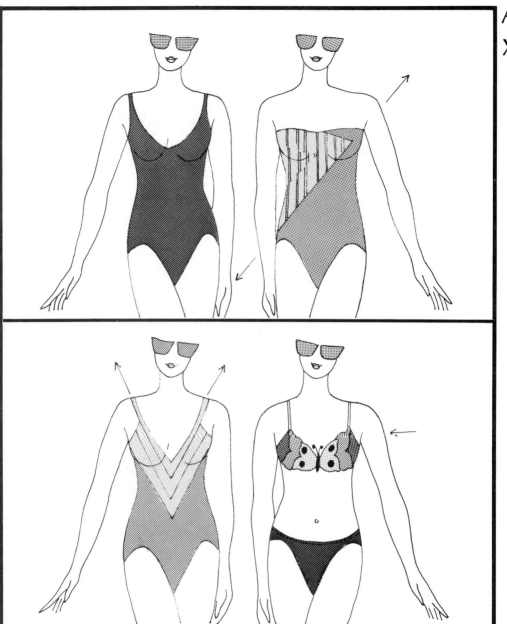

Minimize hippiness

If you're a hippy Body Type (**A, X**) the most basic Dress Thin tactic is a one-piece, dark suit that keeps the eye going vertically. Less basic but equally effective are: the diagonal stripe (top right), an optical illusion that reduces hippiness; the chevron-strap design that balances the **A** type's proportions by adding width above the waist, deemphasizing heaviness below; two-piece suit with print bra to bring the focus *up*.

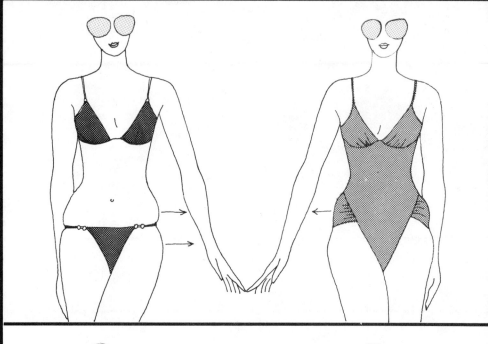

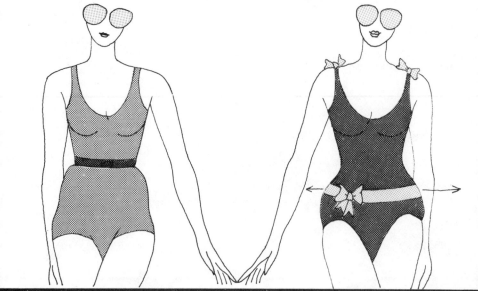

If you're hippy, don't . . .

If you're a hippy Body Type **(A, X, T)** none of these styles is for you. Your Dress Thin eye shows you how the string style emphasizes hippiness, as do gathers at the hips, the belt and the horizontal stripe on these maillot looks. (Styles like those on the preceding page are the ones for you.)

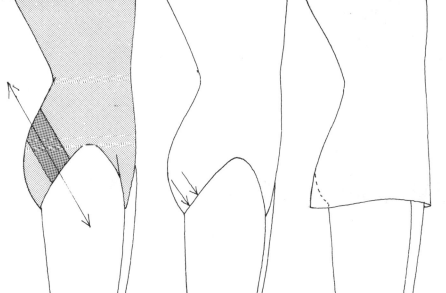

Reduce derrière

Plunging V-backline (top left) appears to reduce the **d** Body Type's derrière; or, use the reverse technique—divert the eye with a *high*-backed maillot. Vertical stripes minimize, and the diagonal design band (below left) seems to cancel the bulge. *Most important:* derrière looks less ample in a style that's cut to keep cheeks covered (below center and right).

d

Too much derrière? Don't . . .

Your well-trained Dress Thin eye can see immediately why your **d** type derrière should not wear anything resembling what I drew on these. (Use the techniques shown on the preceding page.)

Thigh hiders

If you have heavy thighs **(A, X)** there are several ways to skirt the issue. . . . It's more fun to wear a light, unconfining cover-up skirt (or pareo—see page 245) on the beach than to feel self-conscious. Other good ideas are skirted maillots and two-piece suits with shorts.

57

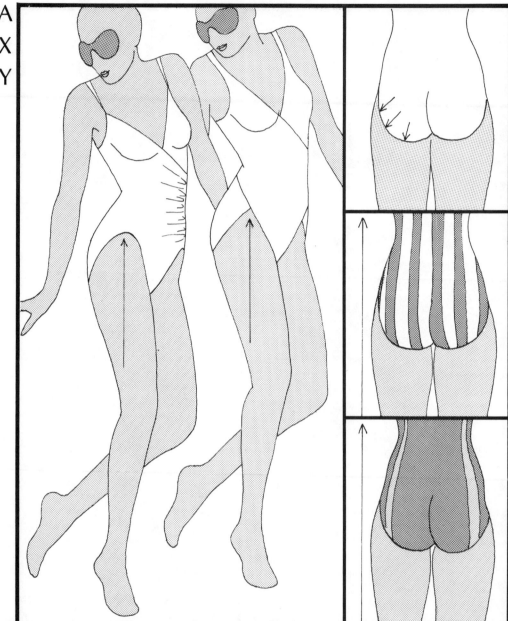

A
X
Y

Thigh-thinners, leg-lengtheners

If your thighs are wide **(A, X)** or your legs are short **(Y),** there's nothing as effective as wearing your swimsuit legs pulled up high toward your hipbones—the diagram on page 38 shows you how. (In back, however, good coverage is essential to minimize the width of your thighs.) Or, choose a maillot with high-cut legs already designed in. Vertical stripes work to thin thighs and lengthen legs, too.

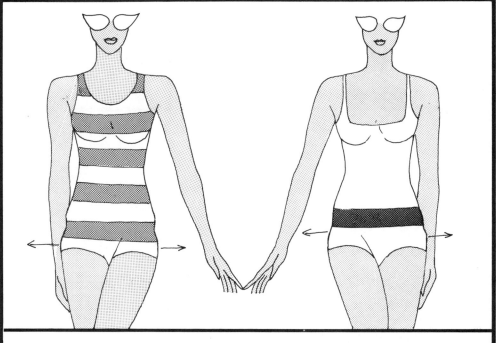

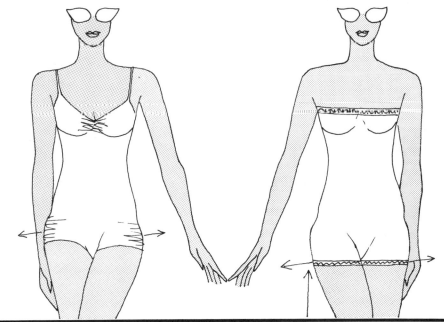

Heavy thighs? Short legs? Don't . . .

Horizontal stripes, shirring and straight-across legline are all anti-Dress Thin if your proportion problem is thigh-width (**A, X**) or short legs (**Y**). See the *right* looks for you on the preceding pages.

2. UnDress Thin and Sexy
Bras, Panties, etc.

Y ou've only just begun to use my System and you've already learned some of my most advanced techniques—the ones that improve your proportions when you're wearing almost nothing, in public. Before we go on to what you wear for all the occasions that call for your fully clothed body, there's another important *un*dressed situation I want to uncover right here. In "intimate apparel," as stores call it, you're wearing less, but *what* you wear means more for three reasons . . .

First, it's *essential* to start from the *inside* if you want to make all the rest of the Dress Thin techniques in this book work most successfully.

Second, when you *take off* your clothes, you don't want to undo the proportioned image you've so carefully created with them on. If you follow my recommendations in this chapter, you can use your intimate apparel to maintain your visually balanced, thinner illusion right through the whole UnDress Thin process—a definite plus if there's someone around whom you care about impressing.

And third, when you look as proportioned and well-put-together in your "underthin's" as you do in your clothes, you'll look and feel sexier, no matter what your personal interpretation of sexy happens to be. It seems to me that the principle is the same for indoor sports as for the others: the more confidence you have, the better you're likely to play.

What is sexy? A math-minded friend figured out that there are 288 possible Body Type combinations within the Dress Thin System. I'm sure that's only the *beginning* of the number of feminine interpretations of what's sexy, not to mention all the masculine ones we'd have to add: "Sexy is very subjective," says fashion stylist Christine Karam. "What it is depends on what kind of man you like." *Every*body's definition is different (take a poll and see).

"What's sexy? That depends on what you like best about your figure," actress Elke Sommer told me. To *be* sexy, explained sportswear designer Carol Horn, it helps to "know how to take advantage of how you're built."

So using your Body Type knowledge will help you UnDress Thin just as it helps you Dress Thin. For instance, "Be aware of the line your panty creates on your leg—it took me years to find a flattering panty, cut to emphasize the length of the leg. Panties and bras that cut into you are *not* sexy," Carol emphasizes. And so do I. The bulges they create are *both* anti-Dress Thin and anti-UnDress Thin. Like any other kind of clothing, no matter how beautiful the style or fabric, if underwear doesn't fit you well, it just can't feel comfortable or even look attractive—much less sexy. (On the very last page of this chapter, you'll find an illustration of proportion-correcting, sexy panties cut like the ones Carol spent years hunting for.)

Ten ways to UnDress Thin and Sexy. Since you're reading this book, I know you care about your image, so I'm sure you'll be glad to hear some new ideas about how to project the best of you in the most intimate of situations (in later chapters, of course, we'll deal with your public image). Here's my collected wisdom—from many discerning sources—for you to use and enjoy.

1. To look and be sexy, be yourself—bras with padding aren't you. Neither is a lot of the hardware or complicated, heavy engineering elements sometimes found on bras.

2. Anything that's hard to *take* off is a turn-off, girdles, especially; tricky bra closures, too. Avoid both.

3. Girdles are also anti-UnDress Thin and Sexy because they inevitably draw attention to your proportion problems instead of to your assets. And even when they do control the bulges you're concerned about, they often create new ones in the process—two more good reasons to take my next point to heart.

4. When you put on *visually* proportion-balanced underwear (as described later in this chapter) you'll see how much more esthetic and sexier you look than you do in overconstructed foundations.

5. If **b** is in your Body Type monogram, make sure the waistline of your panties doesn't emphasize tummy bulge (see the swimsuit bottom illustrated on page 52).

6. Just as in swimwear, horizontal stripes on panties break your line and make you look heavy if you have any lower-torso proportion problems. For the same reason, avoid a garter belt in a color that contrasts strongly with your skintone. (To create a flattering long line, wear a garter belt under a pretty teddy—see page 75—in the same color.)

7. When you take off your clothes in someone else's presence, do *reveal the best first!* If you have great legs, there's no reason not to *start* by taking off your skirt or pants. Be creative—draw attention to your assets! Also consider the three important "don'ts" that follow.

8. For the sexiest effect, *plan ahead*. Don't wear underwear that imprints lines, especially horizontal ones, on your skin.

9. If you *insist* on wearing any sort of lower-torso control foundation, don't show it off; remove it at the same time as your pants or skirt.

10. If you happen to be wearing socks, don't cut the attractive long line of your body by standing around in nothing but. (See Chapter 3.) Slip out of socks before anything.

Dress Thin from the inside: a bra that fits. Pauline Trigère told me that one of the worst errors a woman can make is to put her body in a size 10 when she's really a 12 or 14. If you squeeze into a size that's too small, it will only make you look bigger—and this is true in any fashion category, including foundations. Retailer Bertha Berman, who's been doing a thriving bra and lingerie business in her New York specialty shop, Lee Baumann, for fifteen years, says women think there is some sort of magic about a 34B. The truth is quite the opposite of course, if your size is actually 36C. "Instead of making you look smaller, a bra that's too small for you makes you look bigger. You end up looking as if you have four breasts—two in the middle of your neckline and one on each side of it," she said.

A small size on the tag won't do anything to make you appear smaller—no one sees it but you—yet if you wear the right size in a bra style that proportion-corrects, you *will* Dress—and UnDress—Thin.

In bras (as in any fashion category) good fit begins with the right size, which, happily, you can determine in no time. Use the following two-step method that's recommended by Playtex, Inc.:

1. *Diaphragm measurement for bra size:* While wearing a bra (one that doesn't bind or gape anywhere) stand in front of a mirror and place a tape measure snugly around your diaphragm—where the bottom band of your bra is—and keep the tape parallel to the floor. Note the measurement and add 5 inches. Example: If your diaphragm measures 31 inches, adding 5 gives you 36—so your bra size is 36. If your diaphragm measurement plus 5 equals an odd number (33, 35, etc.), just add 1. Example: 32 inches plus 5 equals 37 inches and adding 1 gives you 38—so your bra size is 38.

2. *Bust measurement for cup size:* Now place the tape snugly around the fullest part of your bust (again, keep tape parallel to the floor). Note the measurement and compare it to your bra size (the diaphragm measurement you just took).

If your bust measures	Your cup size is
up to ½" more than bra size	AA
up to 1" more than bra size	A
up to 2" more than bra size	B
up to 3" more than bra size	C
up to 4" more than bra size	D
up to 5" more than bra size	DD

Normally, the size you just arrived at will fit correctly, *but* whether you're a full-busted **r** Body Type or a small-breasted **i**, it's possible that you'll wear one size in one company's bra and a different size in another's—which does complicate matters. So whatever your size and Body Type, I suggest you take the time to try on a variety of styles, and if an experienced fitter is available, by all means ask for her expert advice.

If you're a busty **r** Body Type, you'll find a good fit visually lifts and minimizes, supporting your Dress Thin effort under anything you wear. Your bra need not be heavy, overconstructed or uncomfortable to give you the lighter, lifted look you want. Note that many underwire bra styles also come in soft cup versions, so try on the same style with *and* without the wire. You may find that the soft cup gives enough support for your figure and is more comfortable. Check the bra list for all my bra style recommendations. When you find the right one(s) for you, it's a good idea to buy several since you may not

Dress (and UnDress) Thin with the right bra

	For full bust r	For small bust i
BRA TYPES	minimizer[1] plunge[2]* sports bra	plunge[2] sports bra demi-bra[2]
CUP CON- STRUCTIONS	molded (no seams) underwire soft cup (no wire)	molded (no seams) underwire soft cup (no wire) bralette[3]
PADDING		push-up[1] contour[1] soft fiberfill[1]
CLOSURES	back hook front hook*	back hook front hook pull-on (no closure hardware)
STRAPS	strapless* halter* convertible* camisole[4] (back adjustment)	nonadjustable (no strap hardware) strapless halter convertible camisole[4] (back adjustment)

[1]This bra does affect proportion but, in *my* opinion, isn't sexy.

[2]This bra is intended primarily to complement certain fashions; its effect on proportion is minimal.

[3]Mostly for coverage; minimal, if any, effect on proportion. Often not cup-sized.

[4]Gives a smoother look under clothes; engineered for breasts that are fuller underneath than on top.

*Bras in this category may or may not offer your figure enough support to improve proportion balance. Support is *not* adequate if you see wrinkles in the bra cup under the point of the breast.

easily find one you like as much if the manufacturer decides to discontinue your favorite. And to preserve the support qualities of its synthetic fibers, wash your bra soon after wearing to remove destructive perspiration acids.

The small-breasted **i** body needs a bra that defines breast contours. What you *don't* need, in my opinion, is heavy padding. Especially under knits, it looks unnatural, which is not Dress Thin in my book, and not UnDress Thin and Sexy, either. A bra with light fiberfill, however, is the equalizer you need if your breasts are significantly different in size. (It's also the answer if you don't want your nipples to show under thin fabrics.)

As Kathy Borgman, who was once my valued assistant and is now design assistant at Vassarette, points out, a pull-on bra is great for an **i** body because there's no hardware to create bumps under your clothes. (In profile, you don't want the bra closure bump under the back of your sweater to rival the size of your breast bump in front!) For my other style recommendations for your figure, see the list below.

If you're an **i** type and prefer not to wear a bra, please note that for running and other active sports, you absolutely *must* wear a running or sports bra. You'll be sorry sooner or later if you ignore my advice. As Marlon Brando said to Maria Schneider in *Last Tango in Paris,* "In ten years you'll be playing soccer with them." In fact, it may only take a few months to do the damage.

For everyone who wears a bra, these important points: you'll never know whether it really fits unless you put it on correctly. After you hook (or pull) it on reach into the cups and center your breasts in front . . . see whether you fill out the bra, or overflow. Position your nipples symmetrically, pointing straight ahead and tilted *up.* You may not have realized it, but if nipples point down, your breasts will *seem* to sag, even if they really don't. Finally, use this simple wrinkle check-up method suggested by Kathy Borgman to determine whether a particular bra gives you correct support for a proportion-balanced look:

- Does bra cup show vertical wrinkles between the point of your breast and the place where the bra strap meets the cup? If so, *your bra is raising your breasts too high for a well-proportioned effect.*

- Does bra cup show wrinkles under the point of your breast? If so, *your bra is not lifting your breasts high enough to improve proportion balance.*

Underthin's from the waist down. As I said at the outset, I hope you'll Dress Thin and comfortably with my proportion-correcting fashion system, rather than wear a heavy, unsexy foundation to cope with a lower-torso proportion problem. My *first* "underthin" choice is a bikini panty with high-cut legline that coincides with the natural bodyline where your leg joins your torso, preventing the panty leg elastic from cutting across fleshy areas to cause anti-Dress Thin bulges. If you're flabby, though, a smoothly fitting brief is better than a bikini. For light control, if you insist, try a "control brief" panty girdle made of a Lycra spandex/cotton blend that's cooler and more comfortable than styles made of all-synthetic fibers. A light panty girdle or control brief is usually not too restrictive but gives a nice lift with molded construction and/or a center back seam for cheek definition. I certainly recommend one of these rather than an old-fashioned panty girdle that squeezes you together and makes you look like a sausage. (Lack of definition is a dead giveaway that you're wearing a girdle.) Use any girdle or all-in-one foundation only as an emergency measure— you've planned on a certain dress for a certain occasion and at the eleventh hour you realize it doesn't fit the way it did when you last wore it.

As noted earlier, a half-slip made of noncling taffetalike fabric is an instant Dress Thin *must* for all Body Types. No matter what the label says, try on the petticoat to make *sure* it's noncling. At the same time, check for bulky gathers at the waist. If the fabric clings anywhere or bunches at the waist, keep trying until you find one that doesn't. A half-slip that fits and hangs properly—under one of the skirt or dress styles recommended for your Body Type later in this book—is the best Dress Thin technique, *not* a girdle.

Underthin' color tactics. Versatile beige and flesh tones are my top Dress Thin recommendation . . . all-beige underthin's rarely show through any color clothes, producing no fattening horizontal bands of conspicuous color. White often *does* show through in bands and makes you look as if you just got out of the hospital, as well. Black is nice under dark clothes, but beige is fine if you prefer to own only one color. If, however, you like to project your Body/Style sense with colored lingerie, coordinate your UnDress Thin and Sexy look by using the most striking color to focus attention on the part you want to show off; for example: a red bra with pale pink half-slip and pale pink panties, both trimmed in red.

P.S. Despite all the different opinions about what's sexy, everyone I polled seems to agree on one point: the smoothest, silkiest lingerie fabrics you can find are the sexiest. No scratchy lace to offend the hand. As Elke Sommer says, "If it feels good, it's sexy."

Minimize full bust with good support, visual balance

Bra manufacturers' "minimizer" styles (top left example) give good support for full bust **(r)** but tend to be somewhat heavy visually. Try some on, but also compare lighter-looking underwire styles (center) and their sister versions in soft cup construction. For an UnDress Thin and Sexy look, balance bust with panty styles that are not too skimpy (illustration at right). NOTE: Color-matching bra and panty is visually lengthening . . . sexier, don't you think?

Full bust? Don't . . .

(Top left to right) Too-small cup size and bra size make full bust **(r)** look fuller and give you anti-Dress Thin bulges in back, too. Bras with nonadjustable straps often give droopy look, and so do your nipples if you forget to position them front and center! Below left to right: Don't wear a white bra that shows through clothes and spotlights full bust. To me, balanced-looking proportions are more esthetic, sexier than this effect. What do you think?

i

Small bust? Choose contour-defining style, balance proportions visually

If your bust is small (i), test each bra style for contour-defining capability by trying on a sweater over it. Camisole plus tap pants lingerie combination gives visually balanced UnDress Thin and Sexy look, as does repetition of neat triangle shapes in bralette and bikini. NOTE: Maintain balance with color-matching bra and panty.

Small bust? Don't . . .

Don't wear flattening sports bra (left) under street clothes if you're small-breasted **(i)** but DO wear one for running and sports. Big area of "brief" style panty style is unbalanced by small bra area—makes small bust seem smaller (right). NOTE: Don't wear lighter-colored panties than bra.

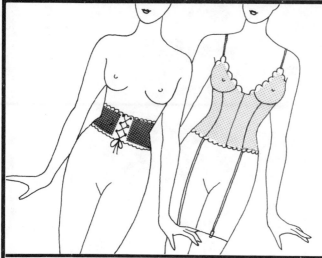

Cinch yourself a waist

If you're a straight-up-and-down **H** Body Type, you can get a waist with a cincher (left) or corselette (right). Some just like them for sexiness.

Light shaping for torso heaviness

For wide-waisted **(H)** or heavy-torso-thin-legs **(T)** proportion problems, body suit (left) made with Lycra spandex stretch fiber smooths torso, helps shape waist. Or, try a high waist brief panty girdle (right).

Light control for profile proportion problems

If your Body Type is **b** (tummy bulge) or **d** (prominent derrière), you may want to try a light-control panty style with tummy panel (left), a control brief panty girdle (center) or smoothing panty with Lycra spandex fiber content (right).

71

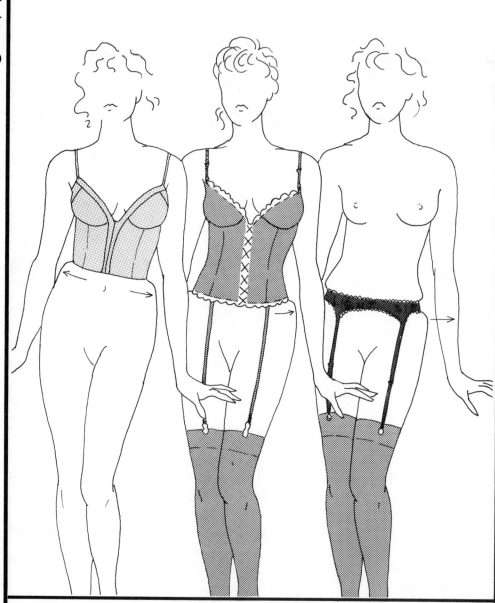

A
X
T
b

Tummy or hips proportion problem? Don't . . .

If your tummy's prominent (**b**) or you're hippy (**A, X, T**), don't wear these potential bulge-causers: longline bra (left), corselette (center), garter belt (right). Intimate apparel styles that fit well look sexier than those that cause bulges.

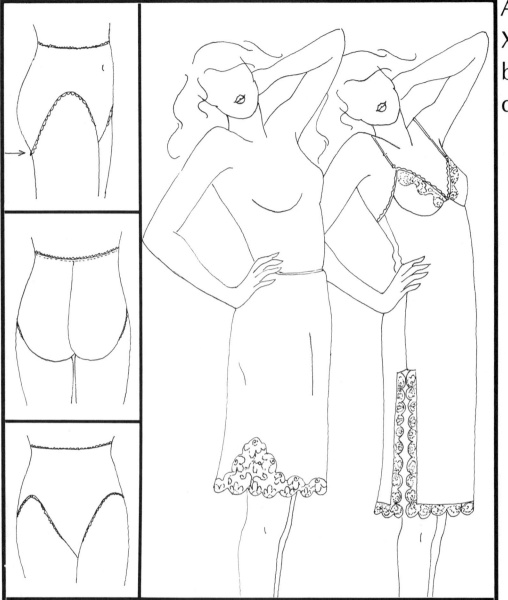

Minimize lower-torso proportion problems

If you have a profile problem (**b** or **d**) or are hippy (**A, X**), here are some solutions: smoothing panty (left) in cotton/Lycra or nylon/Lycra with properly cut legline that coincides with the line where your leg meets your torso in front and under buttocks in rear view; light control brief style (bottom). *Always* smooth out lower torso problems (thighs, especially) with a half-slip under a skirt. A bra-slip (far right) or full slip also helps conceal lower-torso bulges.

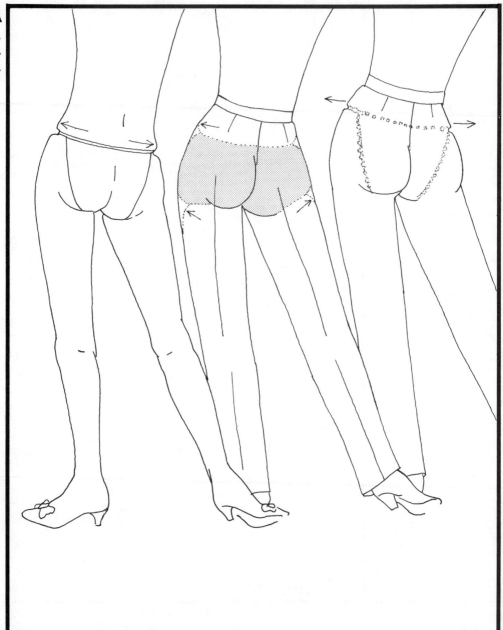

Heavy below the waist? Don't . . .

Lower-torso problems (**A, X, T**) are all aggravated by these mistakes: tight bikini panties (left and center); contrast-color panties or bulky trimmings that show through snug pants. NOTE: Avoid light panties/dark bra combination that highlights heaviness below the waist.

Minimize heavy thighs

If your thighs are heavy (**A, X**) choose: panties with high-cut legline that detours the problem area and lengthens thighs (left); teddy with no elastic to cut in and cause bulge; panty leg control style (right) is suggested as a last resort only!

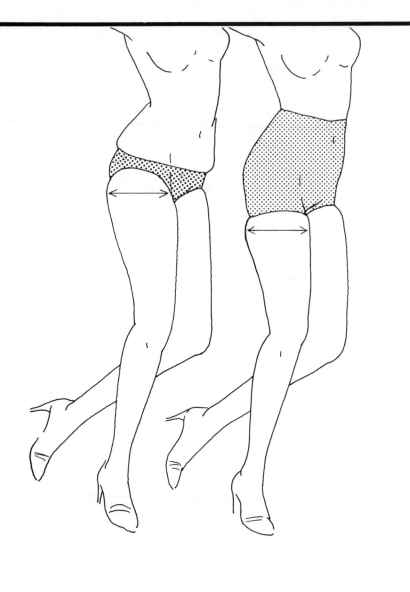

Heavy thighs? Don't emphasize them

Avoid panties with tight elastic (left) and panty girdles with low-cut legs that emphasize thigh bulge **(A, X).**

Proportion-corrector for long torso, short legs

If your Body Type is **Y**, for good proportion's sake do choose high-cut bikini (left), *not* briefs with low-cut legs. The high-cut bikini is also preferable because the legs of brief-style panties often ride up uncomfortably and with bulky anti-Dress Thin consequences, as well.

3. Dress Thin from the Ground Up
Footwear and Hosiery

I'm not being funny when I say you won't make any Dress Thin headway unless you start at the foot. If your proportion-correcting efforts stop at your hemline, your Dress Thin strategy just will never get off the ground. (That's why a full-length mirror is indispensable.) On the other hand—or foot—well-thought-out shoes and hosiery will lift and lengthen your entire bodyline.

Rather than worry about how heavy or how thin your legs are, concentrate on using this chapter to expand your new understanding of the visual relation of your legs and torso. Your Body Type is the *key* to exploiting color, texture and even hosiery construction to make yourself look taller and thinner. And believe it or not, the first step in making your Dress Thin System work from the ground up is *foot comfort!*

The first step. Yes, even though I'm a designer, not a doctor, I'm here to tell you why foot comfort is essential. . . . *Every* step you take critically affects your Body/Style image because your shoes have a pronounced effect on your posture. And as you already know from Part I, you need good posture when you walk, stand and sit to Dress Thin successfully.

According to Dr. Marilyn Moffat, Associate Professor of Physical Therapy, New York University, both poor fit and extremes of shoe styling can cause discomfort that disrupts body alignment. For example, very thin heels don't offer the body an adequate base of support; when you wear them, your muscular activity is totally devoted to stabilizing yourself when you stand and walk, rather than to maintaining alignment. Shoes with heels over two inches high throw your body forward, and you compensate by arching your back. This not only causes a strain on your back, but also makes your stomach protrude, Dr. Moffat points out. So, even if you don't actually have a tummy to begin with, wearing very high heels can easily make you look as if **b** is one of your Body Type initials.

You probably have noticed, though, that high heels give the illusion of longer legs . . . a Dress Thin advantage that's tempting. Is it possible to give in to this temptation without affecting your posture so adversely as to cancel out your leggy gains? My own compromise approach is to try to restrict the amount of time I spend in high heels. I stash low-heeled standby shoes in whatever places I spend long periods of time—in the office, for instance. (As every tall woman who ever fell for a shorter man has discovered, low-heeled pumps are a trade-off worth making. Ask Nancy Kissinger!) I wear my standbys when I'm on my feet a lot. This way, I minimize the muscle fatigue that produces fattening slump.

For long walks on city sidewalks, I've learned to wear rubber-soled running shoes or crêpe-soled styles. Orthopedist William Hamilton says such soles protect the feet by absorbing some of the shock produced when they hit concrete. Dr. Hamilton is also in favor of wearing "flat, casual shoes around the house: sneakers, clogs or wooden exercise sandals. These let you stretch out the tightness in your calf muscles that high heels produce. By wearing flats regularly, you become comfortable with your calf muscles stretched—that's much healthier than being married to high heels as lots of women used to be."

I find that wearing high heels part-time is a workable trade-off, but good *fit* should never be compromised. Nevertheless, Dr. Hamilton estimated that as many as 60 percent of women may wear shoes that are too small. "Don't let a salesperson tell you that shoes will stretch," he emphasizes. Keep shopping until you find the style you want in your correct size. Otherwise, as Dr. Moffat explained, shoes that are too short or have very narrow toe styling force you to "constantly adjust your position to ease the compression wherever your feet are sore. Suppose you have corns on the outer edges of your toes—you'll try to walk on the inner part of your feet and this throws your knees, hips and back all out of alignment."

Achieving balanced foot-leg-torso proportions with shoes. Wearing the highest heels you can find to help you look taller and thinner is not good Dress Thin strategy because of the negative effect such heels can have not just on your posture but on your proportion balance, as well.

When you wear pants, very high heels do improve your torso-to-leg proportions, especially if you're a short-legged **Y** Body Type. Try on a pair of pants and soaring heels—you'll see that your legs appear longer, your derrière higher, *provided* that your pants are long enough to hit your instep and that your shoe-hosiery-and-pants color blend creates a "unified leg" as illustrated on page 83. But be warned—if you spend much time on your feet, the resulting slump will counteract your pants-with-high-heels proportion-correcting tactic.

Your basic shoe rule should be moderation, not only in heel height, but in all aspects of shoe styling. "In the shoe industry, moderate heel height is considered two to three inches, and a happy-medium heel is one that is neither too thin nor one that's positioned too far to the rear of the shoe. Heels that are too thin, too high or set back too far will deprive your torso of an essential proportion base," says Arsho Bagsarian, talented designer of the chic, famous Shoe Biz line. No matter what your height and Body Type, the idea is to "cultivate a sense of proportion about how your heel height affects your total body picture," she suggests. "If you are heavy in *any* part of the torso, a very high or skinny heel will just exaggerate the heaviness above. Since very high heels shorten the foot visually, your body seems supported by a base that's too delicate." Arsho drew an upside-down triangle to illustrate how this minimal shoe "base" appears to maximize the body above it.

In fact, most fashion extremes in shoes tend to be anti-Dress Thin since they negatively affect both proportion and posture. Choose toe shapes that are oval or moderately pointed, rather than ultra-pointy, and avoid very pared-down shoes or sandals both for comfort and good proportion's sake. When you dress up, of course, wear more delicate shoes than usual, but don't choose a style *so* delicate that it fails to balance your body visually.

Extreme shoe styles that are too heavy and too tricky are also anti-Dress Thin because they anchor the observer's eye at your feet, rather than encouraging the eye to move up and down along a continuous leg and bodyline for the thinnest possible total impression. This is true for all Body Type proportions—feet should never seem to go off on their own visually, but always be a part of the *unified* Dress Thin approach to legs which you'll next read about in detail.

The principle for boots is the same. As you'll see in the boot illustrations, the boot that solves the most figure proportion problems is a knee-high style that doesn't hug leg curves but whose straight line from knee to ankle allows the eye to travel uninterruptedly from your foot up. And to keep the line unbroken it's very important that your hem cover your boot top. A sudden patch of knee between boot and skirt is really an anti-Dress Thin eye-stopper—and so are bulging calves at your boot tops! To prevent the latter, choose boots with gores (elastic inserts) or have boot openings stretched until they fit without choking the leg. Note: To be stretchable, *both* boot and boot lining must be leather; synthetic linings won't give.

The unified leg. No matter whether you're about to make a major purchase of shoes or boots—or just to pick up new panty hose—remember to consider your choice in the context of your total head-to-toe proportion picture. Instead of wasting time and energy worrying about big thighs, heavy ankles or whatever, spend that time and energy in front of your full-length mirror, reflecting on what you have learned from your proportion survey.

To create the unified leg, I'll show you how to use what artists call color value. Value simply means *darkness* or *lightness,* as when we say "*dark* blue" or "*light* brown," and a combination of colors that are the same—or close—in value creates unity. So by wearing shoes, hosiery and dress or skirt colors of the same or similar darkness or lightness, you visually link those fashion elements and achieve the lengthening unified leg look that's a Dress Thin basic.

The table that follows shows the best Dress Thin color-value strategy for your unified leg schemes, depending on your Body Type proportions. Double checks indicate the ideal Dress Thin choice; a single check means second best—and NO means anti-Dress Thin!

The Unified Leg

		YOUR BODY TYPE PROPORTIONS		
		Heavy in any part of torso (A,X,H,V,b,d,r) with short legs (Y) or heavy legs	Broad shouldered or heavy in torso with thin legs (T, VT)	Heavy in torso with thin, short legs (TY)
THE RIGHT COLOR-VALUE SHOES + SHEER OR ULTRA-SHEER HOSIERY FOR YOU	LIGHT nude; beige	NO	√√	√
	MEDIUM mocha; suntan; taupe	√	√	√√
	DARK coffee; charcoal; off-black	√√	NO	NO
THE RIGHT COLOR-VALUE SHOES + OPAQUE PANTY HOSE FOR YOU	LIGHT pastels; pale beige; pale gray	NO	√√	NO
	MEDIUM tan; azure; turquoise; rose	NO	√	√
	DARK loden; navy; dark brown; wine; eggplant; black	√*	NO	NO
THE RIGHT COLOR-VALUE SHOES + TIGHTS FOR YOU	LIGHT pastels; pale beige; pale gray	NO	√√	√
	MEDIUM tan; turquoise; azure; rose	√	√	√√
	DARK loden; navy; dark brown; wine; eggplant; black	√*	NO	NO

√√ Best choice   √ Good choice   NO Don't wear
*For your proportions, the most thinning *color-value* choice is dark; whenever possible, choose sheer or ultra-sheer *construction* in preference to tights or opaque panty hose for the best Dress Thin effect.

The illustrations on page 83 show two ways to create the unified leg: with a one-value scheme and with a close-value scheme. The simplest one-value technique is to wear the same color in the same value in shoes, hosiery and clothing (dark brown shoe, dark brown hosiery and a dark brown skirt, for instance). But you can also combine *different* shoe, hosiery and clothing colors and still get a unified effect, provided that the *values of the colors are all the same,* and that the colors all belong to either the warm or the cool color group. In the warm group are red, orange, yellow, reddish-purple, red-brown, yellow-brown, warm (red- or yellow-influenced) beige and warm gray. In the cool group are blue, green, blue-green, blue-violet, bluish-brown, greenish-brown, cool (blue- or green-influenced) beige and cool gray. Black and white are not considered colors and therefore do not belong to either color group. Neutral colors are medium-value and light-value grays and browns with no perceptible reddish or yellow (warm) tinge and no bluish (cool) tinge.

The one-value example at left in the illustration on page 83 combines three colors of the same value from the warm color group. In the right illustration, the close values could be warm pastels, or three neutral close values, including black. To get the true meaning of the illustrations, *squint!* This will show you how close *values* merge—even if *colors* are different—to unify the leg and body. As you experiment with your own unified leg schemes, check them with the Squint Trick. When you squint, the values should merge as they do in the illustrated examples. In plotting unified legs, your scheme could include either classic, sheer hosiery, *neutral shade* panty hose or opaque panty hose or tights in such colors as burgundy or plum. The words "opaque" and "tights" describe hosiery construction and will be explained in the section that follows, which shows you how panty hose construction can help you Dress Thin instantly.

How to use contrast color for Control Point legs. Very few of the **T** Body Types I've known have thought of using their legs as Control Points, but this novel technique works beautifully to balance torso heaviness with bright or light color value shoe-and-hosiery gambits to make thin legs *contrast* with medium or dark clothing shades. This is shown in the contrast leg illustration on page 84.

I knew one **T** type who always wore black from head to toe. Although black dresses were good strategy for her torso, the black shoes and panty hose just made her slender legs look like two little matchsticks emerging from a chunky matchbox of a torso. Her torso actually seemed *bigger* than it really was in comparison to those little wisp legs. The moral of her story is this: If you are a **T** type who's over 5 feet 5 inches, you can wear contrast color shoes and hosiery to *emphasize* your slender legs. With this Control Point strategy, you'll have everyone admiring your legs—and ignoring the fact that you're heavier somewhere else.

The unified Dress Thin leg

A one-value scheme (left) is the ideal approach to the unified leg, giving your figure the most continuity possible. *Squint* at the diagram and note how the values merge into one. This example represents *three different colors that are all equally dark:* red-brown shoes, red-burgundy panty hose and sweater, reddish-purple skirt. (All the colors are from the red-influenced warm group.)

The close-value approach (right) is also effective, providing that you select close values that are *close enough*. To test them, squint! The values should blend—no part should appear to separate itself from the whole. This example could represent the following colors that are close in value: beige shoes, nude panty hose, chino-tan skirt, pastel-yellow sweater. *Or,* the following black scheme: black shoes, off-black panty hose, black skirt, charcoal sweater.

The contrast leg

The contrast leg is a Dress Thin strategy that works well only for the thin-legs-heavy-torso proportions of the **T** Body Type. All other types should use the unified leg technique. The contrast leg should always be achieved with dark or medium-value clothes combined with lighter-value hosiery and shoes (never the reverse) because the light-value color makes legs appear heavier, helping the proportion balance of legs and torso, *and* because their lighter color makes legs function as what I call the Control Point—attracting attention to their own shapeliness and away from a heavy torso.

You can do this conservatively by wearing tan, beige or light gray shoes and hosiery (with clothing colors like navy, charcoal, deep brown or burgundy); or if your personality is fiery—why not red legs with black clothes! *Warning note:* No matter whether you're a **T** or any other type, you should never wear shoes in a lighter color than your hosiery. This causes a stubby-leg illusion that doesn't flatter anyone and sabotages all the best-laid Dress Thin plans.

Not just the **T** but anybody with good, slender legs should use them as a Control Point—to focus attention on them and so divert the eye from liabilities elsewhere. You can do this not merely with color, as I explained, but you also have a whole world of fashion hosiery textures and special "clock" effects at your feet. Why not do as my mother does (she's a **T**!) and collect a wardrobe of interesting textured legs, both dressy and tailored. Use any of the many exciting textures the hosiery industry produces for you. If your ankles are thin and your legs have shapely curves, seamed* panty hose is another way to get Control Point emphasis, but if your legs are very thin, wear texture or clock effects, not seams.

If your legs are slender but you're a short-legged **Y** type, your strategy should be the unified leg, not the Control Point. As I've explained, the unified leg look is the best Dress Thin approach for most Body Types, and to get it you should choose plain panty hose or only minimal texture or pattern—like those illustrated on page 87.

The foregoing recommendations for short legs also apply to heavy legs. And if your legs are short or heavy, *don't* wear panty hose marked opaque, since these are actually semisheer, causing light and shadow "halo" areas that add width. Don't wear large patterns, horizontal stripes or heavy verticals, either.

Socks savvy. When country weekends or sports situations call for socks, minimize heaviness and keep your legline going by wearing *foot* socks, or long legwarmers in the same color as whatever you're wearing underneath them. Or, choose dark knee socks with a dark skirt or shorts. *Don't* wear ankle socks, calf-high socks or socks with horizontal stripes—all of these styles not only emphasize leg heaviness but torso heaviness, too. Also avoid them if you're a short-legged **Y** Body Type, since they cut the length of your legs and your height as well.

How panty hose construction can help you Dress Thin instantly. The wonder of panty hose knit construction is that it's an instant toner. Slip into any panty hose at all, and *voilà*—your derrière, hip, tummy and legline are perceptibly smoother and thinner looking. Even more exciting, though, is that if you choose to put on panty hose marked control top, you can take off a visual five

---

*Only *straight* seams are lengthening! To make sure yours are, just put a dot of rubber cement toward the top back of your thigh. And if you're bowlegged, pass up seams.

pounds just like that. This panty hose construction offers an immediate inexpensive Dress Thin morale-boost: control tops are the fastest crash diet ever invented.

Not as thinning through the torso as control top but more *leg-slimming* are panty hose labeled "support," and tights made with Lycra spandex stretch fiber. These are often constructed without a reinforcement line between leg and panty, which makes them both good choices under high-slit or wrap skirts.

Panty hose labeled "sheer" and "ultra-sheer" offer the least Dress Thin help, but do give your legs a smoother, more toned look than if you went barelegged. Tights show *no* skintone through the fabric, but (confusingly) so-called opaque styles are actually somewhat sheer. As my hosiery illustrations show, after opaque panty hose and tights, sheer panty hose are the best Dress Thin option. The at-a-glance table below gives my Dress Thin panty hose construction recommendations for your Body Type.

Although panty hose called ultra-sheer have a knitted-in smoothness that reduces the cling of your pants or skirt—which is a definite Dress Thin asset— they also tend to bag at ankles and knees, which is not! Ultra-sheer construction is the best choice under pants because its smooth texture reduces cling—pants are less likely to stick to your curves. The sheer panty hose construction rarely bags and wears better than ultra-sheer. It does have a sticky texture that clothes cling to, however, so to Dress Thin be sure to wear a slip over panty hose labeled "sheer."

Dress Thin panty hose construction recommendations

YOUR BODY TYPE PROPORTIONS	Control top	Support	Sheer/Ultra-sheer
Heavy in any part of torso **(A,X,H,V,b,d,r)** with short legs **(Y)** or heavy legs	√	√√	√
Heavy in torso with thin legs **(T)**	√√	NO*	√
Heavy in torso with thin, short legs **(T,Y)**	√√	NO*	√

Unless you need support hosiery for health reasons.
√√ best choice   √ good choice   NO don't wear

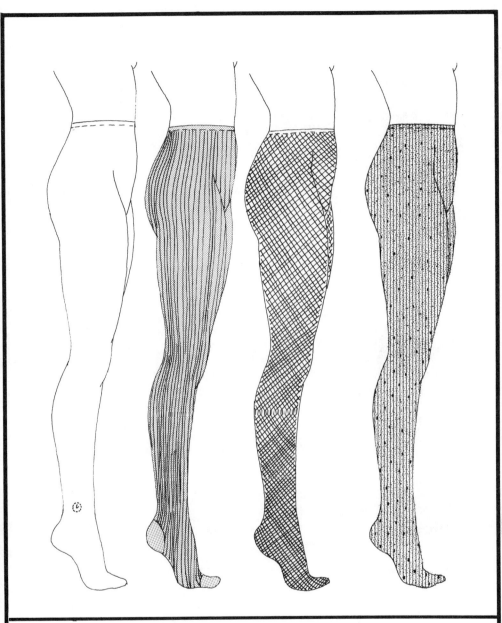

Minimize below the waist with fine hosiery textures

For heavy legs and lower-torso heaviness types **A, b, d, X,** the optimum solution is *no* pattern at all on legs, but you can make life interesting with Dress Thin Fashion Trade-offs if you're careful to choose minimal effects like these. Left to right: tiny clocks, very fine pinstripe, fine fishnet, point d'esprit. If you're a **T** Body Type, *reverse* the strategy shown here—see next page. NOTE: When you want texture, choose textured *sheer* panty hose, *not* textured tights if you're an **A, b, d** or **X** type.

A
X
T
Y
b
d

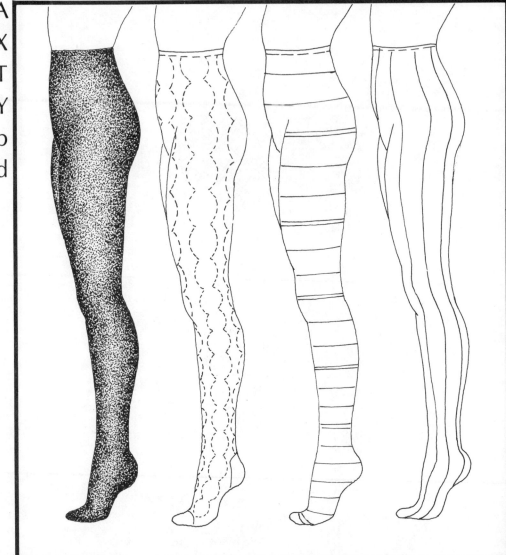

Heavy below the waist? Short legs? Don't . . .
T proportions? Go ahead . . .

If your Body Type is **A, b, d, X** or **Y,** don't wear panty hose marked opaque (left), since these are actually semisheer, causing light and shadow "halo" areas that emphasize your proportion problems. Also don't wear large patterns, horizontal stripes or heavy verticals. If you're a **T** Body Type, however, hosiery styles like these that emphasize leg curves and fill out thin legs are excellent Control Point strategy for you. NOTE: The **T** type should also exploit the contrast leg idea illustrated on page 84.

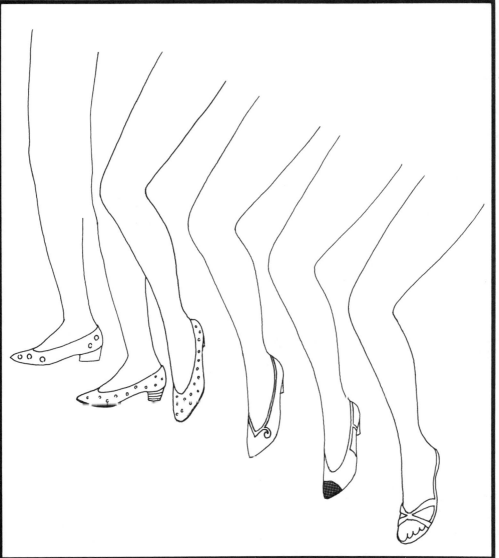

Balance torso heaviness with shoes

To Dress Thin, visually balanced proportions are the key, and shoes can help! If you're heavy above the waist (**r, V**) *or* below (**A, b, d, X, T**), the rule is: be sure your heels look substantial enough to visually balance the legs and torso they're supporting. The lowest heel you should wear is one inch; preferably a chunky Cuban shape (left).

Similarly to heel shapes, toe shapes and sandal straps must be substantial enough to balance heaviness above for Body Types **A, b, d, X**. Best toe shapes are oval (left), moderately pointed or squared. The Chanel toe tip is flattering *except* if your foot is small, in which case the look is stubby and unbalances your proportions. Sandal straps should be medium width.

Balance heaviness below the waist with shoes

Both closed and open shoe shapes are proportion-correcting for heavy legs and for lower-torso heaviness types **A, b, d, X:** pumps (left) with moderate vamps that neither choke the foot nor are too scooped-out; low, sleek boots create a long line with pants, or with a skirt plus textured hosiery in the same color. The volume of a wedge provides good visual support for the body, but choose a well-cut style that tapers slightly into the sole—never one that splays out and visually echoes lower torso bulk. The slingback style (near right) flatters both heavy ankles and delicate ones and lengthens the legline nicely. (For good fit, get a sling that buckles.) Mules give the longest legline of all. (They're safest and stay on best when you wear them without stockings.)

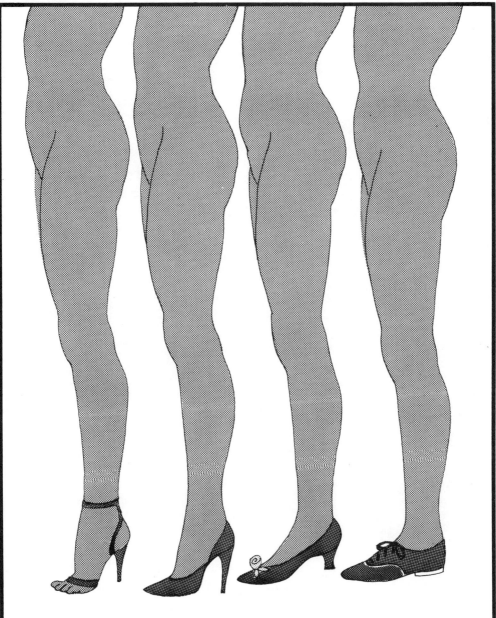

Heavy torso? Don't . . .

Here are several footnotes that can sabotage your Dress Thin effort: very delicate styles; any ankle straps, especially wide ones; extremely pointed toes or extremely skinny straps or heels and flat-flats. Be *sure* to avoid very curvy heels (near right) if you're a very curvy Body Type **(b, d, r, X).** Good shoe strategies for you are illustrated on pages 89 and 90.

Balance heaviness below the waist with boots

Most flattering boot shapes for heavy legs and lower-torso-heavy types **A, b, d, T, X** are knee-high and straight-sided, almost cylindrical pull-on boots. If you have a high instep or wide calf and can't wear the pull-on style (left), then choose the straightest-sided design you can find in a knee-high zipper style. Cowboy boots are also a good choice because of their straight silhouette, well-balanced heel and toe shapes. NOTE: For the longest line, your skirt should just cover the top of knee-high boots; cowboy boots are best with matching or blending hosiery underneath, not contrast-color.

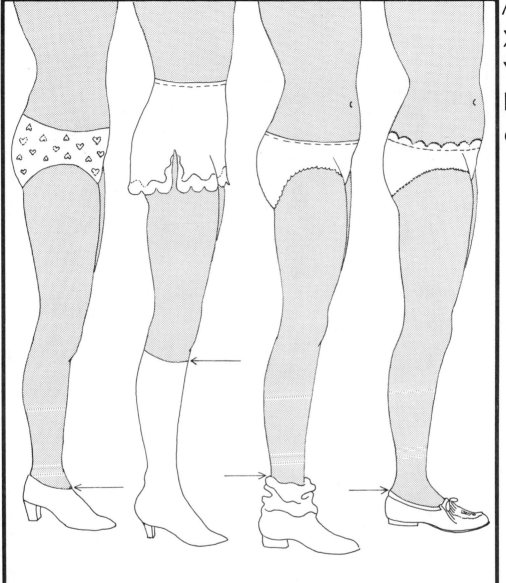

Heavy below the waist? Short legs? Don't . . .

For Body Types **A, b, d, X** with heavy legs and heavy lower torso, and for the short-legged **Y,** these styles are anti-Dress Thin: heavy, "choked" vamp pumps (left), skintight boots (too curvy), cuffed boots (too horizontal), and flats (not lengthening). Boots and shoes that work for types **A, b, d** and **X** are shown on pages 89, 90, and 92. For the **Y** type, see page 96.

Balance T̲ Body Type's slim legs and
heavy torso with socks

When you wear jeans or tights, you can use short legwarmers (left) as some dancers do, to visually balance your slim-leg-heavy-torso **T** type proportions. You can also wear most sock styles, especially in tones to blend with your skin and *contrast* with your clothes. If you have short legs **(Y)** or are the **A, b, d** or **X** Body Type, *don't* wear any of these. Ditto if you're bowlegged.

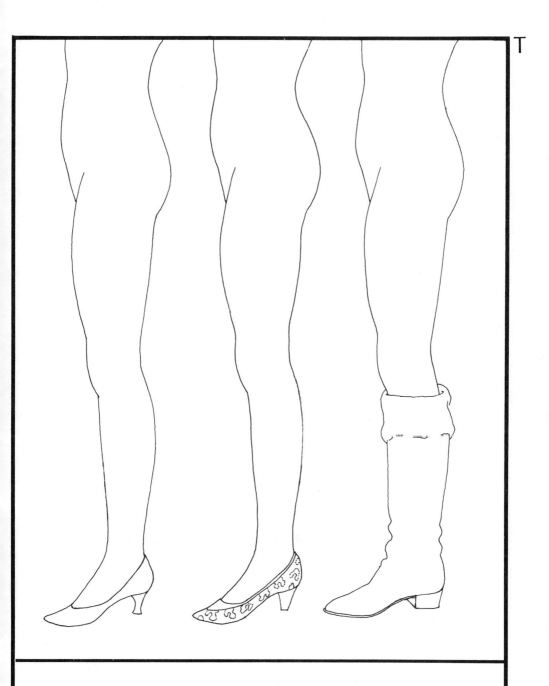

Footnotes for balancing slim legs and heavy torso

Heel and toe shape recommendations in the preceding pages are equally wearable for your Body Type, and you should also follow most but not all of the shoe and boot "don'ts" covered there, too. Exceptions that flatter your thin legs (but which Body Types with heavy legs and heavy torso must avoid) are the following styles: curvy and set-in heels, cuffed boots.

Lengthening footnotes to short legs

Short legs in proportion to torso are characteristic of the **Y** Body Type. To lengthen your legs if you're a **Y,** high heels and delicate shoe styling ideas like these are excellent Dress Thin footnotes: slingbacks, low throatlines (left); backless mules, thin platforms (center); open-shank styles, oval toe shaping. Your best boot strategy is a straight, knee-high style. NOTE: It's essential that your skirt cover the tops of your boots.

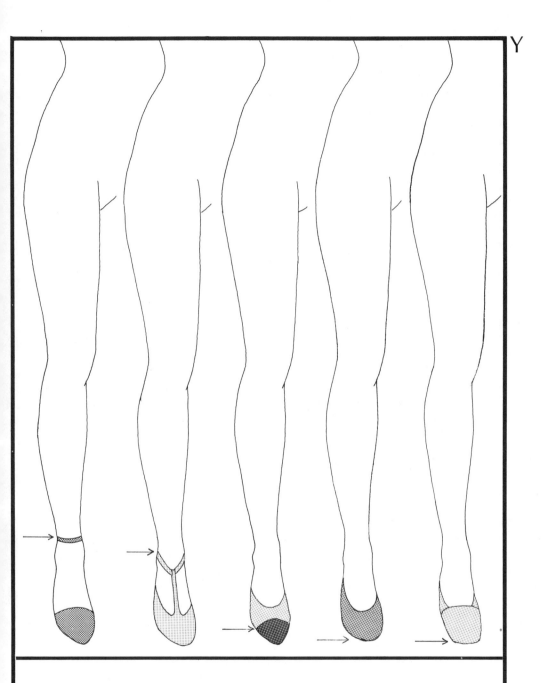

Short legs in proportion to your torso? Don't . . .

When legs are short in proportion to torso, these footnotes shorten the leg even more and work against a **Y** Body Type's Dress Thin effort: ankle straps, T-straps, Chanel-toe styles, round and very square toes. Dress Thin shoe and boot style recommendations for you are on preceding pages. NOTE: See the ''don't'' footnotes for your Body Type on page 93.

4. Dress Thin and Fast
Dresses

You sleep through your alarm and cut your dressing time by half on the very day you want to Dress Thin sensationally for a new client meeting. . . . You get caught in traffic and reach home so late you have only fifteen minutes' Dress Thin time to change for that anniversary dinner date. . . .

When you want to look—and feel—terrific, but you don't have time to try on five skirts to perfect the proportion balance, what you need is the fastest-acting Dress Thin formula possible. You need a dress. Pearl Nipon is a designer who, with her husband, Albert, works in many fashion categories but says her first love is dresses because, "Being a busy lady, I don't want to have to think about putting things together. When you buy a dress, a good designer gives you something that's complete.

"If you choose to, you can accessorize it in a dozen different ways and give it your own identity. But you don't even have to do *anything* with a wonderful dress. It's already done. You don't have to worry, 'Does this go with this?' or 'Does this blouse balance this skirt?' "

A little advance planning is all it takes to ensure that a Dress Thin lifesaver dress is always in your boat. Why not start planning right now, with an unhurried reading of this chapter, taking note of my style suggestions for your Body Type proportions. Then, make your Dress Thin and Fast shopping trip, scouting for a minimum of one with a crisply tailored look and one softer style in fabrics appropriate to whatever season of the year is coming up next.

Selected with the help of your personal Dress Thin consultant (that's me), your two dresses will not only make it easy to get yourself together for any occasion in record time, but also to restructure your proportions for a stunning *instant thin* impression. With all your Dress Thin dress savvy, you'll pick styles that designers like Pearl Nipon have created to solve the proportion problem for you—so when seconds count, you don't have to do it yourself. For example, if you buy a belted style (consult the chapter diagrams to see whether belts are for you) look for *hidden* elastic under the belt. This is a great Dress Thin-and-comfortable feature because with your belt buckled at the right place there is nothing to cut into your waist and cause bulges above or below it, as can happen with constructed waistbands that don't give. And as for those accessories Pearl Nipon mentioned, see Chapter 10 for 25 dramatic ways to individualize your dress.

For the instant Dress Thin purposes of this chapter, what I mean by "dress" is *not* anything and everything found in a dress department; it *doesn't* mean jacket dresses or styles with tops and skirts that resemble sportswear separates. (Chapter 6 is your complete guide to putting together Dress Thin separates. The techniques there will help you assemble multiple parts, regardless of the department—Dresses or Sportswear—in which you happen to purchase them.)

The one-step proportion-problem solution. Any one-piece or layered dress (such as a tunic or overblouse style) that visually unifies the figure by means of a solid color or an allover small print has Dress Thin potential for solving proportion problems. The trick, of course, is to choose the dress(es) that will balance your particular proportion problems, and based on your Body Type, there is a simple, Systematic way you can identify at a glance the Dress Thin silhouette for you. . . .

At any given time, fashion offers a choice of the four essential dress silhouettes listed below. Note that depending on the trends of the moment, certain ones may be more available than the rest, but some styles in each broad silhouette group are always on the market. That's why it's essential not to be a blind trend follower but to develop and follow your *thin*stincts. As Pearl Nipon put it, "Don't buy trendy trends. You can be up to date in something you've owned for three years." As well as be in "better shape," if you choose correctly among these four:

1. Narrow bodice, controlled-fullness skirt*
2. Full bodice, straight skirt
3. Straight chemise silhouette
4. Full caftan silhouette

Depending on where *your* proportions are fuller and narrower, you should pick your dress silhouette to play up your thinner Control Points, and conceal heavier areas. For curvy profile Body Types, a straight chemisey silhouette choice minimizes curves; or, if you're torso heavy, choose a concealing caftan silhouette that dramatizes your face. To zero in immediately on your basic strategy, see the table below, and, for specifics, check the style illustrations later in this chapter.

---

*Skirt may be very full if fabric is sheer.

Instant Dress Thin dress silhouettes

Left to right: narrow bodice, controlled fullness skirt for narrower-above-the-waist Body Types; full bodice, straight skirt for narrower-below-the-waist Body Types; straight chemise silhouette for curvy-profile Body Types; full caftan silhouette for torso-heavy Body Types.

Which Dress Silhouette for Your Proportions?

Dress Silhouette	Your Proportions	Body Type Initials
Narrow bodice, controlled-fullness skirt*	Narrower above the waist	**A, Yi, ib, id, Wb, Wd**
Full bodice, straight skirt	Narrower below the waist	**T, Tr, Hr, Yr, Vi**
Straight chemise silhouette	Curvy profile	**X, rb, rd, Vr, Vd, Vb**
Full caftan silhouette	Torso heavy	**H, HY**

*Skirt may be very full if fabric is sheer.

An important proportion factor to consider once you've chosen your basic dress silhouette strategy is skirt length—and these days, you can consider them *all* because anything goes! The famous French couturière Chanel is credited with the rule that the best skirt length for Everywoman is just below the knee. This is a good rule, and it certainly follows that above-knee lengths should be reserved for sports and for those with flawless legs. I would add, however, that if you have problem legs, you should consider a lower hemline—*except* if you're also a **Y** Body Type (long torso, short legs).

The color-yourself-thin dress formula. When you color yourself a continuous color from shoulders to hem with a single color or an allover print, that's effective instant Dress Thin technique. So in this chapter, we'll *only* consider dress styles in a single color or an allover print. In the bargain, this will give you a chance to discover how an unbroken expanse of color affects your Dress Thin image. You'll also realize that whether you're buying a dress or a coat, the same color-yourself-thin formula applies, because the same shoulders-to-hem expanse comes into play.

I'm sure you've heard that dark colors make objects look smaller and light colors make them appear larger. This basic artist's "color value" concept is useful, certainly, but a deeper understanding of it can add to your Dress Thin expertise. Color and color preference are tied to our emotions, so there is a lot to be said for making color choices based on what makes you happy. Do you choose to face a gray day in a bright dress, or just to blend in with the mood of the weather? Of course, if what makes you happiest is to Dress Thin—then you'll be especially fascinated by the effects that your choice of warm and cool colors can have on your Body/Style image.

Technically, cool colors are those that are dominated by blue, and warm ones those dominated by red and yellow, but the most important Dress Thin point is that cool colors absorb light and therefore seem to *recede,* while warm colors reflect light and therefore appear to *advance.* So it is not only the dark shades that should go into a color-yourself-thin dress wardrobe, but the *cool* ones.

Leaving aside for a moment not only your emotional preferences, but also the color of your eyes, hair and skin, if you don't want your wide dimensions to seem wider, or the prominent parts of your body to appear to stand out more than they actually do, you'll approach a rack of dresses with an eye to *blues, blue-greens, blue-purples, blue-grays, and bluish-browns*—all in dark rather than light shades. You'll avoid the temptation of *red, yellow, orange, reddish-purples, red-browns, and even yellow-greens*. And consider this more subtle but interesting point: if you find pastel shades irresistible, give in to a blue-lavender rather than a pink or an apricot. . . .

As for the emotional aspect of color, let me add that if you are shopping for a new swimsuit, it would make sense to pass up a favorite color in favor of one with more Dress Thin potential. In a dress, however, the pleasure of wearing a color you love—even if it's not the coolest Dress Thin choice—will probably have a more positive effect on your *total* image than a color you're halfhearted about but know intellectually is more thinning. As I said earlier, *if* what makes you feel best is to Dress Thin, then choose your dress colors accordingly. On the other hand, don't abandon a color that's *you* and projects your you-ness if its loss is going to give you the blues!

An important footnote to the subject of color is added by Pearl Nipon. She recommends that when you're on a budget, and therefore can't expect the finest fabric quality in your purchase, you opt for "classic" colors (black, navy, gray, beige, burgundy) rather than off-beat ones that will draw attention to the fabric of your dress.

Dress Thin with the fabrics of illusion. "I think wearing delicate fabrics makes you look thinner. . . . It takes away that chunky look, so you're just sort of floating. Sometimes I do it with antique dresses. They're so soft, they soften what's there and visually you just can't tell what's you and what's not." So says Ellen Sideri, president of Shull, Sideri Associates, and a savvy fashion professional who's been refining her own Dress Thin style over a period of years, and has her techniques down so pat that only her masseur knows for sure that her Body Type is a classic **A.**

If you're a romantic like Ellen, go shopping for antique clothes and see what you can turn up. For a narrow-above-the-waist Body Type, you might find the right silhouette in an antique dress made of filmy silk or sheer handkerchief cotton. Curvy-profile type? Hunt for a 1920s style chemise in sheer silk (be sure the chemise barely skims your hips—if this silhouette hugs anywhere, kiss your Dress Thin strategy goodbye).

If modern is your mode, of course the range of fabric possibilities for your Dress Thin silhouette is wide. Even when sheers are inappropriate, the softer and drapier the dress, the more you Dress Thin. A Dress Thin dress must *move*. Avoid anything stiff. Here are some drapey fabric suggestions to start you off:

Silhouette	Fabric ideas
Narrow bodice, controlled-fullness skirt	rayon/cotton jersey silk or synthetic silk broadcloth
Full bodice, straight skirt	cashmere blend crêpe de chine
Straight chemise silhouette	wool jersey rayon challis
Full caftan silhouette	wool crêpe Qiana* knit

*Du Pont registered trademark.

One last point, but a crucial one: under sheers, a slip or half-slip is obviously essential. But under *any* of the fluid fabrics, your slip is just as vital. Don't attempt to Dress Thin and Fast with fabric clinging to your curves. It takes only fifteen seconds to put on a noncling half-slip. I timed it.

Shoulders-and-bust-minimizing sleeves, necklines

Dolman sleeve-V-neckline-straight-skirt combination (left) is good camouflage for upper-body breadth; jumper straps minimize by breaking up the expanse; cowl neck (right) brings focus *up* to your face, and neat set-in sleeve is the best Dress Thin sleeve construction.

Big shoulders or bust? Don't . . . Small on top? Do . . .

A close-fitting jewel neckline (left) emphasizes breadth of shoulders and bust, as do gathers or tucks anywhere above the waist. Ruffles add fullness at bust; halter style (right) exposes big shoulders and focuses the eye at bustline. These are all anti-Dress Thin if you're big on top, but are good proportion-correctors if you're small above the waist (**A, i**).

Big shoulders or bust? These sleeves are anti-Dress Thin

The combination of a high neckline and dolman sleeves above a full skirt (left) is the worst one I can think of for heavy upper-body proportions. Also exaggerating to broad shoulders or bust are puffy sleeves of any kind, and raglan construction (right) that creates bulk just where you don't want it. If you're a small-breasted **i** type, these aren't for you either—too much fabric calls attention to proportionally small upper torso.

Full bust? Don't emphasize it. Small on top? Maximize . . .

If you're full-breasted **(r),** a strategic bit of cleavage is fine, but spilling-over décolletages (left) are not. Fitted sweater dresses, especially in clingy knits, are too revealing; wide belts and Empire styling (right) make bust look bigger and are therefore *good* choices if you're small on top **(i).**

107

Create a waist or balance lower-torso width

If you're an **H** Body Type (straight-up-and-down), here are three ways you can create the illusion of a waist. The *same* three tactics are effective balancers for the **A** type's narrow-above-wide-below proportions. Choose: styling that's belted or fitted at the waist and bloused above it (left, center) or a dress with shoulder pads or shoulder detailing to create the breadth that makes the waist appear smaller.

Camouflage wide or short waist; tummy bulge

If you're a wide-waisted **H** type, a short-waisted **W** or have a tummy **(b),** all of these are effective disguises: blouson (left); overblouse, tunic; Empire (right).

H
X
Y
b

Proportion-correctors for mid-body; short legs

To equalize too-curvy **X** proportions or lengthen short legs **(Y)** and bypass wide waist **(H)** or tummy bulge **(b),** these are excellent tactics: a chemise style (left) in a medium to dark color-value solid or an allover print motif no larger than the last joint of your pinky; simple body-skimming cut; top-to-bottom buttoning style.

Shift focus to correct short or wide waist

To lengthen a short waist **(W)** and divert attention from a wide one **(H),** direct the eye *up* with shoulder and neckline details (left, center), or *down* with body-skimming, low-waistline style (right).

Mid-body proportion problem? Don't mark it . . .

If your proportion problem is mid-body, don't focus attention on it with belted styles, revealing center pleat detail, or two-color dress with light-value skirt. Focus on the preceding pages for good Dress Thin dress strategy. NOTE: If you can't *resist* a belted style, a narrow, matching belt is a possible compromise.

b
d

Disguise tummy, derrière!

Profile Body Types with prominent tummy **(b)** or derrière **(d)** can use these styles to disguise the proportion problem: short tunic (left); belted overblouse or peplum (style must blouse, *not* be fitted above the waist); blouson (right).

b
d

Profile proportion problems? Don't . . .

If your tummy **(b)** or derrière **(d)** is prominent, all of these are anti-Dress Thin: narrow-torso dropped-waist style (left); midriff-fitting style; fitted sheath (right).

Lower-torso proportion correctors

If your Body Type monogram shows heaviness anywhere in the lower torso (**A, H, T, X, b, d**), here are two styles that correct proportions by lengthening and two that do it with asymmetrics: narrow chemise made of thin, flat fabric (left) works especially well for heavy-torso-thin-legs **T** proportions; tunic style (underskirt prevents fabric from clinging, smooths over all bulges); asymmetric seaming style; surplice that slims midriff with its asymmetric wrap and creates focus at small waist Control Point for **A** and **X** types.

Minimize lower-body heaviness

Unless one of your Body Type initials is **r** (full bust), you can wear a full-skirted Empire dress (left) and use bust outline Control Point to divert attention from wide waist **(H, T)** or hips or thighs **(A, X)** and from prominent tummy **(b)** or derrière **(d).** Or, exploit the camouflage potential of: tent style; flared tiers of flimsy, fluid fabric; or body-skimming style (right).

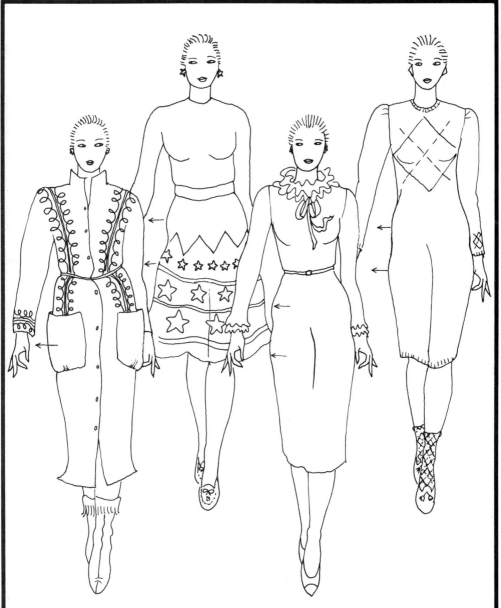

Heavy below the waist? Don't . . .

If your proportion problem is thigh or hip width **(A, H, T, X)**, don't emphasize it with poorly placed pockets (have bulky ones in side seams cut out and sewn closed), or with detailing in lower part of skirt. Narrow, fitted-torso dress and sweater-knit style reveal hip and thigh problems, as well as tummy **(b)** and derrière **(d)** bulges. See the proportion-correcting dress styles for you on the preceding pages.

Short legs? Don't . . .

If you're a short-legged Body Type **(Y),** horizontal lines are your Dress Thin enemy. *Avoid:* border treatments (left); flounces (even *one* flounce); low-placed blouson and dropped waistline (right).

5. Dress Thin
Power Plays
Suits

An executive in a major record company tells me that her boss memo'd women employees on the subject of proper office attire: *More jeans and fewer suits,* he decreed. Apparently, the suit's power as a symbol of organized authority was damaging the company's image—turning off rock stars too laid back to sign up with such a gray-flannel outfit. Meanwhile, paradoxically, in a far-out corner of the rock scene, men and women artists both have begun *performing* in tailored suits. Clothing their kinkiness in the straightest-possible uniform creates a bizarre contrast that they and their fans seem to relish. Or could it be that the groups just want to Dress Thin!

We all know by now that a suit has the power to rocket a woman to the heights of corporate success—but did you ever realize that if you buy *the right suit for your proportions,* you'll acquire the *ultimate* Dress Thin super weapon?

Of course, any complex and powerful mechanism is expensive, and this one is no exception. Very possibly, you'll invest nearly as much in a suit as you would in a coat—especially since women's suits are not altered free, as are men's—though alterations are certainly as crucial to the success of a woman's suit as to a man's. I can only assure you that your Dress Thin suit will be worth all the shopping hours and dollars you spend on it. To guide you in selecting it, I have put together this chapter with the same kind of care that a tailor lavishes on a fine garment.

While you're on your way up the success ladder in certain industries or career areas (sales, for example), you may be subject to dress pressure that dictates wearing suits full-time, and matched suits at that. Take it from a designer—to avoid a boring, Meter Maid look in a matched suit is as challenging an assignment as any you're liable to meet in management. If you try to "dress for success" in a computer formula programmed by a "wardrobe engineer," chances are you'll end up with something that suits a computer phantom but not your body, let alone your personality.

The *good* news, however, is that your in-depth understanding of your own proportions plus the Dress Thin tailoring and style information in this chapter will net you the suit(s) that will give you visibility in the crowd of dress-for-success paper dolls, both male and female.

To impress your "fellow" executives and achieve what's been called equality of image with the best of them, remember this: a man at the top is bound to recognize a well-tailored properly fitting suit when he sees it. He should—he wears one every day. To ensure that your suit jacket is the most successful Dress Thin proportion-maker in your wardrobe, I went to the workrooms of Jhane Barnes. Jhane's precocious career as a tailored-clothing designer began in the true province of great tailoring, men's suits, but now her prized label is found in custom-quality suits for both women and men.

The two sets of checkpoints that follow were worked out in consultation with Jhane and Eddie Di Russo, her master tailor and pattern-maker. In the first list are fourteen vital *fit* checkpoints to watch when you try on a jacket. In jackets as in nonprecision-tailored clothes, wrinkles and stress lines are not just anti-Dress Thin, but also sure signs that a fit problem exists where the pulling happens. The second checkpoint group consists of ten key proportion-corrector style hallmarks to help you zero in on the right jacket fashion idea for your Body Type.

Dress for successful proportions: tailoring and fit. Eddie Di Russo picked up the first tool of his trade—a thimble—when he was eight years old, and it wasn't long before he grew to understand this simple yet vital point. *If the shoulders and the collar of a jacket fit properly, problems elsewhere can normally be corrected by a competent tailor.*

It happens, furthermore, that fit problems in shoulders and collar require an expert tailor to solve, and even then are often too time-consuming, complicated and expensive to be worth tackling. Here, then, are the fit checkpoints, most of which are corollaries of the basic premise above. Wherever possible, a recommendation is included as to whether an alteration should be undertaken. Obviously, though, alterations require a tailor's expertise and advice. So, *either* buy your suit in a store with a resident tailor or move heaven and earth to locate a good tailor and then cultivate him or her.

1. If the collar stands away from your neck, the jacket is not cut for you. Find one that is.

2. Wrinkles at the back of the neck may be the result of stooped shoulders. Ask your tailor to advise you about the feasibility of moving the collar back slightly.

3. If a jacket seems to slip backward—feels as if it's falling off your shoulders—*don't* try to readjust. This one will never work for you.

4. If there's a dimple below the shoulder pad, the jacket is too broad-shouldered for you. Get a smaller size.

5. The armhole seam *must* coincide with the place where your arm joins your body. If it doesn't, ask your tailor whether he can correct it.

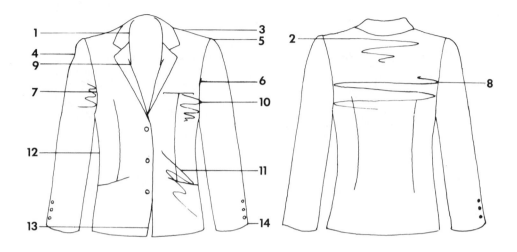

6. If you have trouble moving your arms, too much fabric in the chest could be causing the problem just as easily as too-narrow sleeves. Ask your tailor.

7. If sleeves wrinkle above your biceps, sleeves may be set in too far back. A good tailor can reposition sleeves.

8. If jacket pulls across the back of the shoulders, you need more room there. Find a better match for your proportions.

9. If lapels gape, this jacket is probably too small in the bust. Find one that isn't.

10. If you notice stress lines over the bust, the jacket is too small in that area and the cut may not be compatible with your proportions. Find one that clearly is.

11. If you see diagonal stress lines like these, the jacket's too snug in the waist and/or hips. Your tailor can correct this, provided there's enough seam allowance in the jacket.

12. Jacket waist should *coincide* with your own. If the jacket waist is *above* yours, the jacket will flare out, exaggerating hips, thighs and derrière. Try to find a better cut for your proportions.

13. If jacket pulls open, you need more room in the hips. No problem for your tailor provided the jacket has enough seam allowance.

14. Correct sleeve length is just below your wristbone. (A little shorter if you want to show a pretty cuff.) This is not only right from a classical tailoring standpoint, but also gives your arms a graceful line.

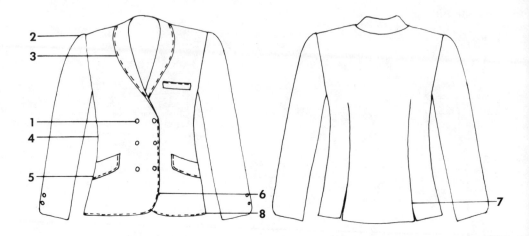

Now that you have an idea of all the complex mechanics and expensive workmanship that go into a jacket, you can appreciate why, as Eddie Di Russo says, a tailor handles the finished product as tenderly as if it were a newborn baby. It's important also to realize, Eddie adds, that your jacket will undoubtedly need careful alteration of some kind, just as a man's usually does. After all, the pattern is based on one set of measurements, not all of which are likely to be identical to your own.

Dress Thin suit styling checkpoints. No matter what your proportion problem, a suit jacket can camouflage it, minimize it or balance it. Here are the *basics* of how this works; of course, specific suits are diagrammed in detail later in the chapter.

1. A proportion-corrector for most upper-torso, lower-torso and mid-body problems is double-breasted buttoning. It minimizes by breaking up your torso area.

2. Shoulder padding is the proportion-helper that balances lower-torso heaviness and is *the* authority reinforcer that lends stature to all Body Types (as every man learns the first time he's ever fitted for a jacket). Even if you're a broad-shouldered **V** type, a style with judicious shoulder padding is a must.

3. If you're a broad-shouldered or busty Body Type **(V, X, r)**, or short-waisted **(W)**, Dress Thin with narrow lapels. If you're small on top **(A, i)**, medium-to-narrow lapels are the best-proportioned choices.

4. If you're an **r, V** or **X** Body Type, note that an ultra-fitted jacket waist emphasizes full bust, short waist, broad shoulders and hips: Dress Thin with gentle mid-body fit. For an **H** type, a very fitted waist gives curvy illusion.

5. Bulky patch or flap pockets emphasize short-waistedness **(W)**, tummy **(b)** and hippiness **(A, T, X)**. Dress Thin with inconspicuous pocket styling.

6. If your Body Type is **A, X** or **T,** *curved* hemline of classic jacket style echoes and emphasizes your thigh and hip curves (this is especially obvious when this jacket is worn with pants). Shorter, *squared-off* styling is therefore a better choice for **A, X** and **T** types.

7. Back vents are dangerous for lower-torso proportion problems of **A, b, d, X** and **T** bodies. Check the rear-view mirror with care before you buy a vented jacket to be *sure* the vents don't gape.

8. Hipbone-length jacket offers better proportion balance than longer styles for the lower-torso heaviness of **A, d, X** and **T** types and doesn't pad your curves with more fabric, either.

9. If you're a **Y** Body Type, a two-button style with the bottom button left open makes your torso appear shorter and your legs longer.

If your work or lifestyle doesn't impose rigid dress-code demands, you can profit from the authoritative aura that a suit creates while you also enjoy the greater fashion freedom suggested by the range of suit silhouettes—including pants suits—illustrated in this chapter. Pants suits are anti-Dress Thin if your proportion problem is lower-torso weight, but if your Body Type is **Y** you'll enjoy the leg-lengthening, torso-shortening power of a straight-legged pants suit with a short jacket. If you wear one, here's what you should know about the correct pants length for optimum proportions:

1. When worn with high heels, your pants should hit your instep in front, slanting down to no more than ⅜ inch longer in back.

2. If you're wearing your pants suit with heels lower than an inch, your pants should "break" slightly (look at a well-tailored man's) over your shoe top.

If you follow these two recommendations, you'll avoid the awkward, anti-Dress Thin look that results when pants are too short to give the illusion of a long, unbroken line.

A matchless Dress Thin technique. As I said earlier, if you're on the way up in an industry or on a career path that dictates matched-suits only, you can and should capitalize on the Dress Thin potential of jacket cut and detailing. But if you've already *arrived* or if no computer-style dress requirements limit your suit fashion options, then the *non*matching suit is your Dress Thin oyster. And what a varied and tasty "diet" you can make of it, for there are as many delicious ways to proportion-correct with nonmatching suits as there are good designers and interesting fabrics.

With the nonmatching suit technique, you simply make your selection according to your Body Type, using *fabric interest* to divert attention from problems and balance your proportions. (Of course, don't neglect good fit and do follow my style recommendations for your Body Type, too.)

1. *To balance heavy upper-torso proportions and camouflage waist and tummy:* Choose a suit with a patterned, textured or light-colored skirt and a jacket with the reverse characteristics (solid, flat or dark fabric).

2. *To balance lower-torso problems, lengthen short legs and disguise small bust:* Choose a suit with a patterned, textured or light-colored jacket and a skirt with the reverse characteristics (solid, flat or dark fabric).

Matched or not, a suit with Dress Thin superpower cannot be made of stiff or bulky fabric, or ultra-textured or oversized in pattern. The most carefully chosen Dress Thin cut won't work unless equal attention is paid to fabric. *Medium-size* plaids and *vertical* stripes can be adapted to the "matchless" proportion-balancing technique just described. Look for flat fabrications like gabardine (in winter or summer fibers) rather than three-dimensional weaves like curly poodlecloth, bouclés or fuzzy mohair that add width to the body. Look for thin, drapey materials such as wool crêpe, as opposed to stiff, bulky ones like cavalry twill or wide-wale corduroy.

Ideally, choose solid-color fabric or the subtlest pattern effects such as heather and nondirectional, tiny tweeds. You might go as far as small patterns like minihoundstooth checks, pinstripes and herringbones; even for proportion-balancing strategy, these are preferable to bold stripes and plaids.

Comfortable, easy-traveling knitted suits tempt many women, but should be resisted if you have *any* lower-torso proportion problem. Body Types with upper- or mid-torso heaviness may proceed with caution and both eyes on the three-way mirror! Choose a flat, jersey-stitch knit—*never* clingy ribbed constructions, nor stiff anti-Dress Thin polyester knit fabrics.

The Dress Thin power play suit partner: your blouse. You need a Dress Thin blouse to back up your Dress Thin suit enterprise, and here's the trick to selecting the right style: An open-V look at the neck is lengthening to every Body Type, and length is the effect you should aim for. Other style alternatives that lengthen are dropped-cowl necks, softly bowed and stock-tied blouses. The illustration on page 143 in Chapter 6 shows a variety of lengthening blouse styles for successful Dress Thin suit partnerships.

To emphasize the V shape created by your blouse neckline, the *color* blouse you choose should contrast with your suit. With one button buttoned, this V-shaped insert of contrasting color reinforces the lengthening lines of your jacket lapels, keeps the observer's eye on a vertical track and breaks up body width—all in the same Dress Thin power play.

Reproportion upper torso, heavy middle and short waist

Hip-length suit jackets with vertical details minimize full bust **(r)** and broad shoulders **(V)**, lengthen short waist **(W)** and conceal tummy bulge **(b)**. Notice vertical emphasis of V-neckline jacket (left), funnel-neck style, braid-trimmed Chanel-influenced look and double-breasted blazer. With any of these, wear straight or tapered pants; straight, A-shaped, or gored skirt.

Full bust? Broad shoulders? Don't . . .
Small bust? Do . . .

If you're broad above the waist, don't emphasize bustline **(r)** or shoulders **(V)** with raglan sleeves or crew neckline (left); wide lapels; shoulder detail or ruffles (right). Also avoid pants and skirt silhouettes that underscore curviness: abbreviated pants (left); low-flare skirt; flounced skirt (right).

All jackets shown are good tactics for you if you're the small-breasted **i** Body Type, but avoid jewel necklines.

Full bust? Too-curvy X̲ proportions?
Wide or short waist? Don't . . .

Don't draw attention to full bust **(r)** or heavy middle **(H, T)**, exaggerate too-curvy **X** torso, or shorten a short waist **(W)** with these styling elements: bolero jacket, circle skirt (left); ultra-fitted jacket, bunchy dirndl; patch pockets, belted jacket, flared pants. Also avoid high-waisted pants and skirts. Your best suit strategies are the ones on page 125. NOTE: To save a belted jacket you already own—just leave it unbelted or tie belt in back.

H

Tactics to create a waist

If your Body Type is **H,** you can create the illusion of a waist with one of these jacket designs plus tapered pants or your choice of *any* skirt. Norfolk jacket (left); multipocket safari style; short, classic fitted jacket; wrap-and-tie (right). NOTE: For the waist illusion strategy to work, shoulders must be padded and necklines V'd.

Disguise and balance heavy lower torso

If you're heavy in hips or thighs **(A, X)**, tummy **(b)** or derrière **(d)**, disguise the weight with one of these jacket styles and *balance* it with shoulder padding. Options include: saddle-shoulder boxy style (left); straight blazer with braid trim to draw eye up; controlled-fullness blouson that has epaulettes for shoulder emphasis to balance lower torso, and is long enough to cover tummy **(b)**. Team these with straight-leg or pleated pants; modified straight or gored skirt. NOTE: Modified straight skirt *appears* straight but is actually wider at the hem. See Chapter 6, page 139.

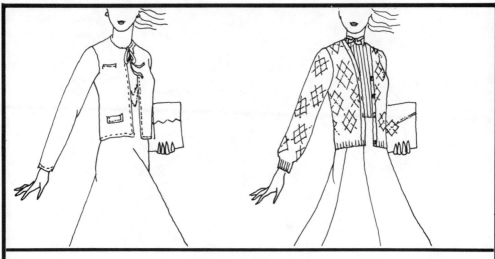

Minimize lower torso

To minimize width anywhere below the waist, the cardigan's straight lines are ideal; to deemphasize hips, jacket should end just above or below, but never *at* hips' widest point. Woven fabric cardigan (left) works best with straight-leg pants; controlled dirndl, A-shaped or gored skirt. If you yearn for a sweater suit, here's your best Dress Thin interpretation: straight (not fitted) jacket plus gored skirt, both in smooth jersey without any clingy ribbing. NOTE: A noncling slip is a *must* under jersey.

Lower-torso proportion problem correctors

Clever construction of these well-tailored fitted jacket styles helps reduce pronounced curves of the **A** and **X** Body Types, as well as tummy **(b)** and derrière **(d)** profile bulges. For the **T** Body Type, jacket fit adds definition to heavy torso. Best partners for Chesterfield style (left) and blazer look (right) are straight-leg pants; modified straight, straight or gored skirt.

¾-length camouflages heaviness below the waist

Body Types **A, T** and **X** can camouflage hips and thighs, while profile tummy
(b) and derrière **(d)** problems are corrected with these ¾-length jacket styles:
topper (left) and other long jackets with gored A-shaped or straight skirt, or
straight or tapered-leg pants. For Dress Thin effectiveness, make sure cardigan
(right) hangs straight; does not pull open across hips.

b
d

Derrière or tummy bulge? Don't . . .

Profile Body Types **b** and **d** should avoid short battle jacket style (left) that exposes *and* echoes bulges below it, especially when worn with pants. Belted styles; waist-seaming and peplum designs (right) are all anti-Dress Thin, particularly when teamed with a pegged skirt or pants. See proportion-correcting suits for you on pages 129–131.

Balance heavy hips and thighs with shoulder emphasis

For Body Types with weight in hips and/or thighs **(A, X, T),** a shoulder-emphasis jacket plus a gored, A-shaped or modified straight skirt or straight or tapered pants is the proportion-correcting equation. Extended-shoulder long jacket style (left) ends below widest part of hips; asymmetric styling (right) brings focus to shoulders which are padded for additional emphasis; shorter extended-shoulder jacket (center) has tapered waist, also works well with pleated pants or circle skirt.

Heavy below the waist? Don't . . .

No matter where you're heavy below the waist, shaped jackets make the problem obvious—especially with a pleated or tapered skirt (right) or tight pants. Rounded jacket hem and belt (left) emphasize bulges below them; leg-of-mutton sleeve curves (center) visually repeat your own, calling attention to what you'd rather camouflage; low patch pockets not only add bulk where you want it least, but also interrupt your bodyline, making you look dumpy. Power your suit strategy with styles like the ones on pages 129, 130, 131 and 133.

Create the illusion of longer legs

If your legs are short in relation to your torso **(Y)**, good strategy is to let your suit correct your proportions. Ideal jacket designs are the hip-length classic style (left) and bolero (center), especially with high-waisted pants. If you're also busty **(r)**, choose Chanel-inspired look (right) or classic, rather than bolero. NOTE: Skirts should end no lower than the knee; pants hem must hit your instep to create the longer-leg illusion successfully.

6. Dress Thin Connections
Separates

Just the opposite of a matched suit with its predictable aura of authority is the separates approach to projecting *any* mood or image you choose. With separates you can plug in a new clothes personality daily if you want—and still Dress Thin. That's why I call these most creative Body/Style elements "connections."

"How do I feel? Who am I today?" With a well-stocked separates wardrobe, anything is possible: Choose your image and connect! If you want to, separates will help you be wildly avant-garde today . . . sexy tonight . . . conservatively classic tomorrow. Sound too exhausting? Then keep your *theme* constant but create different variations on it whenever the spirit moves you. . . .

To some, the infinitely expressive potential of separates may seem like *too much* fashion freedom; sometimes women find it a bit intimidating. *Where to begin?* The answer, as always when you Dress Thin, is *with your Body Type.* And happily, because it *is* systematic, you can use my Dress Thin guide to simplify the selection process. It steers you easily to styles that work for you and eliminates the ones that don't. Make your connections accentuate your assets and express your individuality—both at the same time.

"Once you know your body," says sportswear designer and consummate fashion individualist Carol Horn, "then you can buy *pieces* instead of pre-planned outfits. You'll find you love some pieces more than others, but since this way of dressing is a continuing process, everything will always work with something else you own. So don't be afraid of clothes—experiment, break out of the mold of habit. The dressing room is a place where you can make all the mistakes you want and no one will see you.

"*Start* by concentrating on what cut works best for your proportions, what fits best," Carol advises. "Get to the point of not worrying much about what's fashionable. If you have a good sense of your body and your life, your confidence shows and that 'look' is *always* in."

You may find that good connections happen most naturally with a few pieces that you're comfortable in any time you put them on. If so, switch them around to create your personal "individuality uniforms." As you'll see in this chapter, especially with separates, one way some Body Types can Dress Thin is by letting their proportions—rather than fashion—determine the right skirt length for them. In addition to their attractive flexibility, with Dress Thin connections, you needn't spend a lot because you can collect and recycle them endlessly. I've had some of my favorites for ten years or more! This is where creativity counts more than money—and this is the chapter that makes the most creative connections simple for every Body Type in the book.

Making Dress Thin connections by silhouette. The *relationship* of your separates silhouettes to one another is the basis of the Dress Thin connections system, and later in this chapter you'll find a series of blueprints for creating those relationships successfully, according to your Body Type. But first I want to illustrate for you the shapes—or silhouettes, as fashion people call them—that are most important to your Dress Thin proportion-making connections.

Especially when it comes to what we elegantly refer to as bottoms (skirts and pants) fashion terms are anything but scientific, and are sometimes vague. This is because fashion is a cyclical business, and when the same silhouette returns in a new cycle, fashion writers often like to give it a different name. Interesting new names make fashion more romantic and fun to read about, keeping the reader and the writer both from falling asleep. A new name also helps give an old fashion new life. For instance, maybe you still have some of what used to be described as culottes, or gaucho pants, in your closet, but when the style comes back as a "divided skirt," you decide you have to have one of *those*.

The truth is that styles are almost never revived without being revised in some way—that's what helps keep *designers* from falling asleep! Nevertheless, you can make your culottes work when divided skirts are in. The essential thing is whether they work for your proportions—not what they're called. When you look at my pants and skirt silhouette glossary, you'll see that it's organized in six visual groups to help you concentrate on the shape of things. It's the shape, not the name, that determines whether a silhouette can correct your proportions. The same six groups appear in the silhouette list that follows the glossary and tells at a glance the Dress Thin and anti-Dress Thin bottoms for your Body Type.

Dress Thin Body/Style details. Depending on your proportions, there are both Dress Thin and anti-Dress Thin fine points about style silhouettes that can help or hinder all your separates connections. Once I call your attention to these styling details, you'll find they're easy to recognize. A few may seem subtle, but most are obvious as soon as you begin to see in terms of proportion. Your Dress Thin eye will pick them right out in your closet now, and whenever you go separates shopping, as well. They are illustrated on pages 143–149.

Glossary of Skirt and Pants Silhouettes

Full skirts and pants. Left to right: circle, full dirndl, tiered, multigored, open pleats, unpressed pleats, harem pants, baggy trousers.

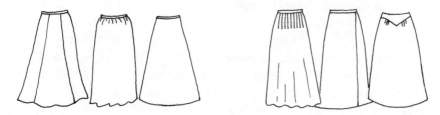

Controlled top-fullness skirts. Left to right: 4–(6) gore, controlled dirndl, A-shape, stitched-down pleats, wrap, yoked skirt.

Controlled top-fullness pants. Left to right: flared, pleated, culotte, yoked.

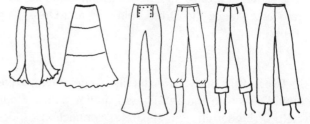

Low-fullness skirts and pants. Left to right: trumpet, flounced skirt, bell-bottoms, knickers, pedal-pushers, above-ankle pants. Note: In the last three pants styles, foreshortening *has the same effect* on proportions as low fullness.

Modified straight skirts and pants. Left to right: plain, wrap, dirndl, pleated straight-leg pants. Note: Modified straight skirt *appears* straight but is actually wider at the hem, which improves proportion balance *unless* your lower-torso heaviness is very severe. Consult the three-way mirror!

Straight skirts and pants. Left to right: plain, wrap, straight-leg pants.

Tapered skirts and pants. Left to right: tapered/pegged skirt, tapered pants, capri pants, toreador pants.

NOTE: In almost all cases, "pants" styles shown are also available as jeans.

As you do whenever you study any of my Style Guide illustrations, follow your initials to the separates details I recommend for your Body Type. You'll discover the proportion reasons why some of your tops and bottoms are favorites while others don't earn their keep. I'm willing to bet *my* favorite sweater that you'll find many of the latter in my anti-Dress Thin Details illustrations.

Anti-Dress Thin Details aggravate the proportion problems indicated by the Body Signs on the page, so you're taking a big risk if you buy something with details I describe as anti-Dress Thin for you. Instead, go for all the proportion-*correcting* Dress Thin Details for your Body Type—your Dress Thin eye will quickly appreciate why they make such an attractive difference.

The Right Pants and Skirt Silhouettes
for Your Body Type

| YOUR BODY TYPE | Pants & Skirt Silhouettes | | | If in Doubt |
	Best	Second-Best	Don't Wear	Don't Wear
Broad or heavy upper torso **r, V**	Controlled top-fullness skirt Modified straight skirt Straight skirt	Controlled top-fullness pants Pleated straight-leg pants Straight pants	Full skirt or pants Low-fullness skirt or pants Tapered skirt or pants	
Short waist or tummy bulge **b, W**	Controlled top-fullness skirt Modified straight skirt Straight skirt	Controlled top-fullness pants Pleated straight-leg pants	Full skirt or pants Low-fullness skirt or pants Tapered skirt or pants	
Heavy below the waist **A, d, H, T, X**	Controlled top-fullness skirt	Modified straight skirt	Full skirt or pants Low-fullness skirt or pants Straight skirt or pants Tapered skirt or pants	Controlled top-fullness pants Pleated straight-leg pants
Short legs, long torso **Y**	Straight skirt Tapered pants	Controlled top-fullness skirt Modified straight skirt Straight pants Tapered skirt	Full skirt or pants Low-fullness skirt or pants	Controlled top-fullness pants Pleated straight-leg pants

How to Choose Contrast-Color Separates for Good Proportion Balance

YOUR BODY TYPE	Best Color-Value Top	Best Color-Value Skirt or Pants	Don't Wear
Broad or heavy upper torso **r, V** Short waist **W**	dark	medium	light or bright color-value top
Tummy bulge **b**	medium	dark	light or bright color-value top, skirt or pants
No waist **H**	light, bright or medium	dark	same color-value top as skirt or pants
Heavy-torso-thin-legs **T**	dark	dark	light or bright skirt or pants
Heavy derrière **d** Narrow-above-the-waist-wide-below **A**	light, bright or medium	dark	light or bright skirt or pants
Small waist-wide-above-and-below **X**	Close-value separates plan is best. Wear lightest color-value above the waist.		
Short-legs-long-torso **Y**	One-value or close-value separates plan is best. Wear lightest color-value above the waist. (With one-value plan, add contrast color *accessories*.)		

If one of your Body Type initials offers a range of "best" color-value possibilities (e.g., "light, bright or medium") but another indicates only one (e.g., "medium"), then for good proportion balance, be guided by the initial that LIMITS your choice.

Dress-Thin-and-Colorful connections. "Women are often afraid of mixing colors," designer Carol Horn points out. "It doesn't have to *match*. Instead of a beige top, a beige bottom and a beige shirt-jacket, why not brown, pink and tan?" Why not, indeed! Once again, the real secret of good connections is confidence. To build confidence in the kitchen, a good cook starts by learning some techniques. Creating recipes on one's own comes with more experience. And in color as in cooking, techniques are yours for the practicing.

In my "Dress Thin from the Ground Up" chapter on shoes and legwear, you saw how one-value and close-value color schemes both work to create the "unified leg," and how the "contrast leg" strategy makes Control Points out of slim and pretty legs. I explained that not only dark, but also cool, colors are Dress Thin because both appear to recede, whereas light and warm colors both seem to come forward. In a parallel way, the intensity of colors also affects their Dress Thin potential: brights come forward, while dull colors recede.

Of course, the blindfold way to make Dress Thin connections work is simply to stick to all-dark values from head to toe, but this is not a very interesting use of separates, nor does it exploit the full potential for projecting an individual image or expressing a mood. It's more fun and just as effective to use the size-changing illusions that contrast-value pieces can create. Here's an example of the effect contrasting values can have on a Dress Thin separates scheme: If you're a busty **r,** and you wear a white shirt *alone* with a dark skirt or pants, the contrast is anti-Dress Thin because it makes your whole upper torso appear bigger. But if you *add* a cardigan sweater, a shirt jacket or a long vest in a dark or medium-value color, you balance proportions and get a thin look. The table on page 141 is an at-a-glance color-value guide by Body Type, and a quicky preview of what the chapter will illustrate in depth.

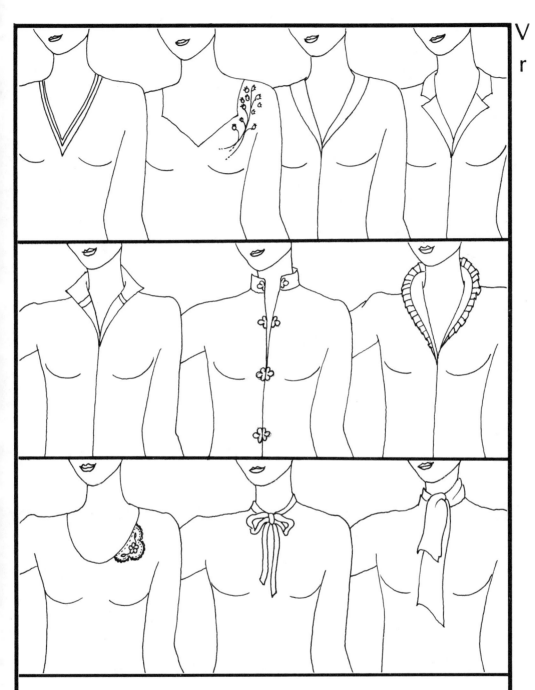

Dress Thin Details: necklines

V-shaped neckline openings (with or without lapels) lengthen all Body Types, especially the broad-shouldered **V** and busty **r.** Second-best are U-necks (bottom left). Droopy bow and stock-tie styles (bottom right) are best if you don't want to wear an open neck.

143

Anti-Dress Thin Details from the waist up

If you're a heavy- or broad-above-the-waist Body Type **V** or **r** (or if you have a short neck or double chin), avoid everything shown here. If you have no upper-body problems, all except the too-tight blouse (bottom right) are acceptable choices. For *most* flattery, see the Dress Thin Details pages marked with your Body Type letter.

Dress Thin Details: sleeves

These are the best sleeve options to help minimize upper-torso heaviness (**V, r**) and heavy upper arms.

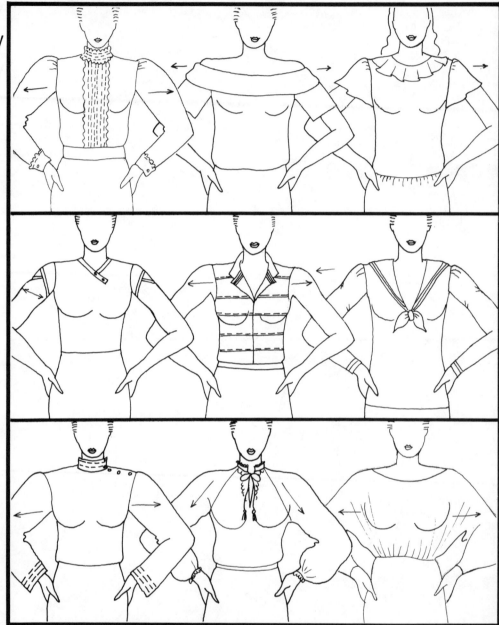

Anti-Dress Thin sleeve treatments

All of these sleeve treatments emphasize upper-torso width (**V** and **r**) by revealing heavy arms, cutting the arm at the wrong place or echoing bust fullness. If you're small-breasted *and* your arms are thin, sleeves in the top row are *good choices*.

If you're busty (**r**) or short-waisted (**W**), sleeves like these exaggerate the proportion problem. (If you're small-breasted [**i**] these are no help.)

Dress Thin Details: sweater fabrications

The airy lightness of lace and pointelle knits (left) makes them good choices if you're busty **(r)** or have a waist or tummy proportion problem **(b, H, T, W)**. More good choices: lightweight sweaters—nothing heavier than Shetland—and flat jersey-stitch knitted tops.

Anti-Dress Thin sweater styling

If you're busty **(r)**, hippy **(A, X, T)** or have a wide waist or tummy bulge **(H, b)**, avoid bulky or balloony sweaters, clingy ribs (center) or short, tight sweaters.

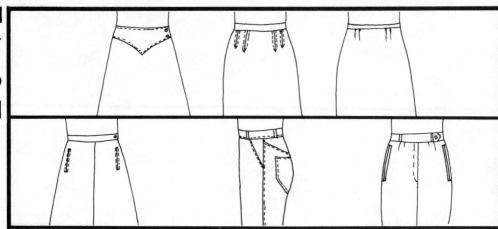

H
T
b
d

A
X
H
T
b
d

Dress Thin Details from the waist down

Look for smooth detailing at and below the waist of skirts and pants if your tummy or waist is heavy **(b, H, T).** Unpressed pleats (far right) should be minimal, or none at all; pockets also minimal, or none at all. And if your derrière's curvy **(d),** flat styling in front and back makes derrière less obvious in profile.

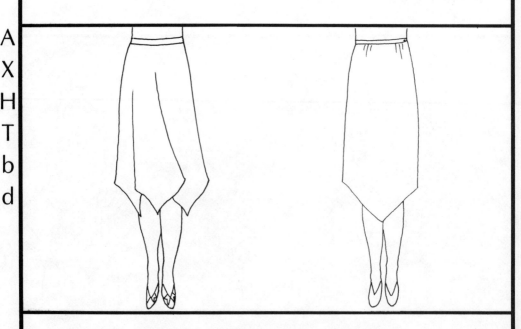

Dress Thin Details: handkerchief hems

Handkerchief hemline is a nice proportion corrector for lower torso heaviness **(A, b, d, H, T, X)** as well as for the short-legs-long-torso **(Y)** problems.

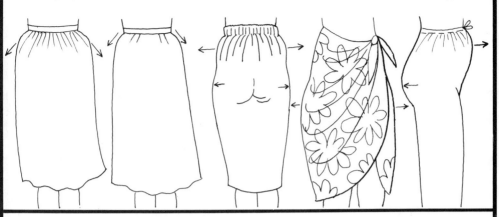

Anti-Dress Thin Details from the waist down

Mid-body proportion problems (b, H, T) are aggravated by bunchy gathers, unpressed pleats, elastic, sarong-tie and drawstring waists. (If you had *no* tummy, these would be the best ways to make you look as if you had one!)

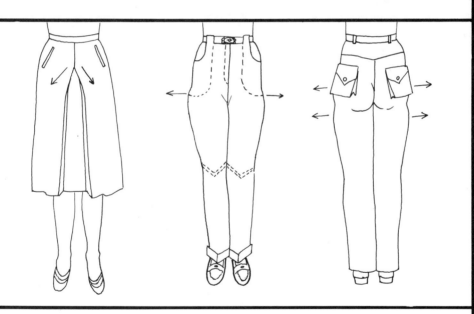

Anti-Dress Thin Details: pleats and pockets

Inverted pleats like these (left) are dangerous for lower-torso heaviness *unless* they fit perfectly. When they pull open they emphasize heavy hips and thighs (A, X, T) as well as tummy (b) and derrière (d); short legs, too (Y). Only long legs, skinny hips and sleek thighs can wear conspicuous pockets like the examples at right.

Anti-Dress Thin Details: pants legs

Long-torso-short-legs **Y** Body Type's pants should not have cuffs, knee-seams or patches that make legs appear shorter. Also, don't roll up pants legs or wear them shorter than instep-length. These are only for leggy proportions.

Minimizers for upper-torso weight

Vertical emphasis and unbroken torso line are effective tactics to counteract top-heaviness. Do it like this: cardigan (left) to establish the vertical, V'd blouse to reinforce it and straight-leg pants to keep it going right to your shoes. Nonclingy sweater with V-neckline and set-in sleeves continues into controlled skirt (no fullness at hip, minimal width at hem) for a lengthening total effect. In shirt example at right, lightly shaped shirt reduces top width and V'd skirt yoke brings eye down. NOTE: Dark color value or cool color for tops is good Dress Thin strategy. Shirts are best in noncling fabrics.

V
X
r

Disguise upper-torso heaviness and too-curvy X̲ Body Type proportions

V neckline plus open vest plus straight-leg pants or controlled-fullness skirt are good disguise tactics for full bust **(r)**, broad shoulders **(V)** and too-curvy proportions of **X** type. Open shirt even saves a too-tight sweater. Or if your sweater is too tight, keep it from clinging by wearing a cotton shirt underneath (right). Wear your controlled-fullness skirts just below the knee to prolong the Dress Thin vertical. NOTE: One-value or close-value color plan emphasizes verticality, too.

Broad shoulders? Full bust? Don't . . .
Small bust? Do . . .

Bulky styling above the waist broadens bust and shoulders; for example: breast patch pockets, shoulder gathers, leg-of-mutton sleeves, blouson fullness and ruffles. But also avoid skirt and pants styles that echo your breadth above the waist: hip patch pockets, wide belts, bunchy gathers, balloony pants. Pegged, short skirt (right) emphasizes derrière curve that echoes prominent bust. NOTE: Avoid light color-value tops with dark bottoms. If your bust is small **(i)** you can maximize it with these top styling details and with light color-value tops, but use these bottoms only if you have *no* lower-torso problems.

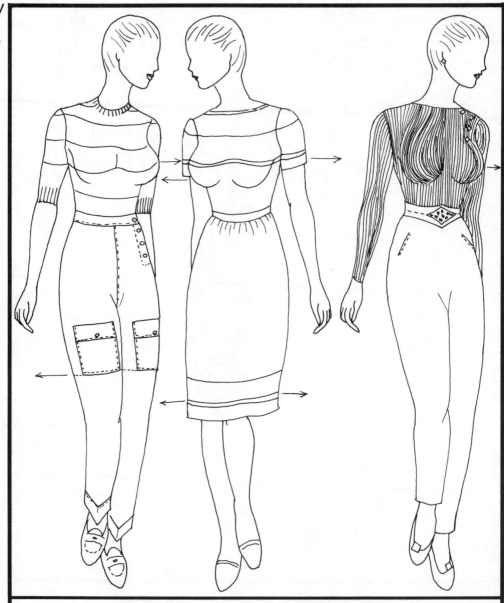

Upper-torso heaviness? Don't . . .
Small bust? Do . . .

Horizontal patterns above the waist and snug or curvy tops are anti-Dress Thin for you if you're a busty **r** or broad-shouldered **V** type. Also, don't compound the problem with jeans styling that interrupts the leg or with horizontal-emphasis skirts. Tight sweater (right), especially a ribbed one, emphasizes bust curves, and tight pants exaggerate the problem.

Proportion-correcting ideas for short waists; disguises for wide ones

Easy blouse and sweater styles are good starting points for schemes that solve waist proportion problems for **W, H** and **T** Body Types. Add controlled skirt style or straight-leg pants. For example: wear shirt as open jacket (left) to top tee shirt or blouse that ends below waist. Long, heavy sweater (or tunic) works especially well with tapered or tight pants (center) *if* you have no lower-torso proportion problem. Dropped-waist skirt choice (right) plus shirt worn bloused will lengthen short waist, hide wide one.

Short or wide waist? Don't . . .

Body Types **W, H** and **T** should avoid dumpiness-producing styles like these: high-waisted pants or skirt styling (left) especially with short vest or jacket; fitted shirt worn tucked in and with collar closed plus open-pleated skirt; tight, waist-length sweater plus full skirt style or any wide-leg pants. (Even if you had *no* tummy, you'd risk getting one by wearing an open-pleated skirt!)

Create a waist or reduce bulky waist

An **H** body can solve the no-waist problem with connections that minimize above the waist and create width below (left) or the reverse (center and right). Shoulder padding also helps give the illusion of a relatively smaller waist. Double-blouse technique (left) creates V-shape that breaks up width for both **H** and torso-heavy **T** types; bloused top belted into narrow pants or skirt style (center) helps lighten both **H** and **T** bodies, as does blousey top (right) over narrow pants. NOTE: Strategic color choices to reinforce double-blouse technique are bright or light-value for underneath shirt, dark-value or cool color for both skirt and outer shirt.

157

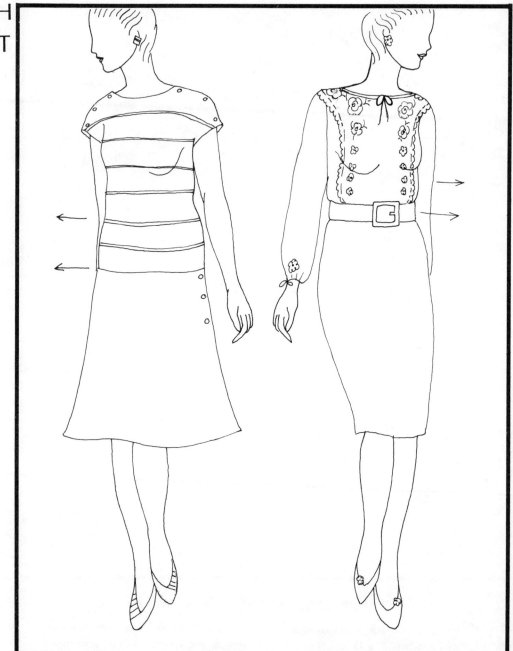

No waist? Bulky torso? Don't . . .

If you have no waist or are torso-heavy **(H, T),** avoid horizontals in the upper-torso area: stripes, boat necklines, wide belts. And notice how a pegged skirt's narrow bottom (right) emphasizes the width above it. Also avoid wearing close-value light colors for both top and bottom.

Strategies to disguise mid-body proportion problems

Layered looks and hipbone-length body-skimming tops are good camouflage strategies for the **b** type's tummy as well as for wide-waisted **H** and **T** bodies. Layered examples include sweater set over straight skirt (left) and vest layered over tucked-in shirt plus straight pants. Any sweater with fullness (style at right) should stop *above* tummy so fullness above it makes tummy bulge less noticeable. Wrap skirts are great tummy hiders; any flare skirt style works if it has *no* top fullness. NOTE: To one-value or close-value colors for tops and bottoms, add light-value or bright color interest in the inner sweater or short layer, but *only* if you don't plan to remove your top layer!

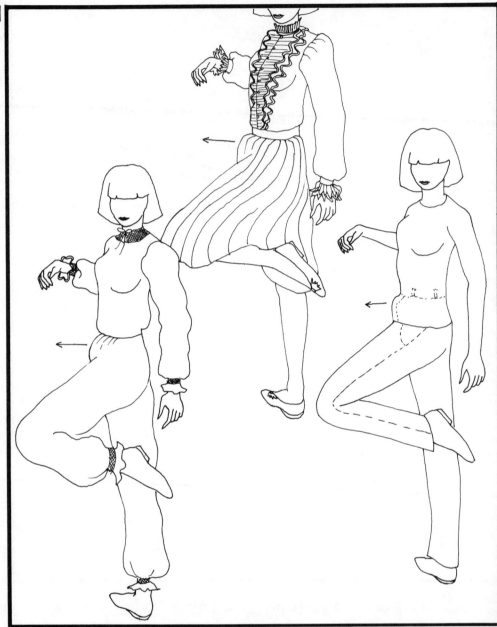

Heavy middle? Don't expose or exaggerate it

If your tummy bulges **(b)** or your midriff or waist is flabby **(H, T),** don't choose styles that echo or call attention to the problem. Therefore, no balloony peasant blouses or harem pants (left); no ruffles or pleats to stick out (center) and no tops or bottoms that are form-fitting in the middle. Also no zippers or fly plackets that don't lie flat; no tight waistbands and no conspicuous buttons in mid-torso (for example, on thirteen-button sailor pants).

Proportion-correctors for lower-torso problems

For proportion problems below the waist, well-chosen top emphasis is a good balancing solution. For example: a bulky sweater (left) that ends at hipbone, or any blouse or sweater with *shoulder padding* or top interest to bring the eye *up* (right). Or, you can hide the problem by wearing a skirt style with stitched-down pleats. Soft-fullness blouse (right) plus skirt that flares from yoke will disguise heavy hips, thighs, derrière. NOTE: In these schemes you can see how close-value color technique works to help deemphasize lower torso.

Proportion-correctors for lower-torso problems

Long-line tops and bottoms correct lower-torso problems with concealing and balancing strategies. For example: lanky sweater plus A-shape *calf-length* skirt (left); long-line vest or cardigan sweater with straight-leg pants and noncling shirt or sweater; easy, hip-length sweater over easy culottes that conceal lower-torso weight. NOTE: Here, bright or light color-value tops plus dark-value bottoms support the silhouette balance that minimizes lower torso.

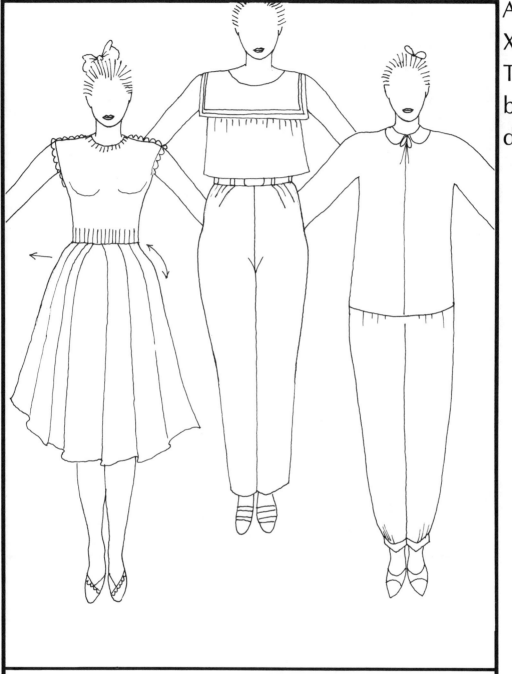

Bulges below the waist? Don't . . .

If your tummy, derrière, hips or thighs bulge, don't wear: a waist-length sweater (left) especially with a wide skirt in a heavy fabric; pants with pleats that slant outward and short, flared top; shapeless tops with shapeless bottoms.

A
X
d

Proportion-correctors for hips, thighs, derrière

Controlled-fullness styles camouflage hip, thigh and derrière curves of Body Types **A, d** and **X.** And by adding shoulder emphasis, **A** and **d** types get good proportion balance. For controlled fullness, choose pleated straight-leg pants, yoke pants style with pleats, or controlled dirndl skirt (right). To emphasize shoulders, use shoulder padding, pleats (center) or sleeve fullness. For curvy **X** proportions, blouse with vertical detailing (right) makes a good connection with controlled-fullness style below. NOTE: Pleats give extra room in pants, so you may wear a size smaller than usual in a pleated style. Lower-torso proportion-corrector separates work best with cool or dark color-value bottoms, bright or light color-value tops.

Curvy hips, thighs, derrière? Don't . . .

As any mirror will confirm, **A, X, d** and **T** Body Types must NOT wear tight pants, jeans or pegged skirt styles at all. Ever. No cheating. So *of course* you won't wear them with a skimpy top! As you saw on the previous page, pleated pants may be a good choice, but take a long honest look in the mirror to be sure. (You may see that any pants style is anti-Dress Thin for you.) If you do buy pleated pants (or a dirndl skirt), pleats must never slant outward from waist, and pants cut should *fit* derrière so as not to bag, as shown at right. NOTE: Beware of tight jeans that make you appear thinner when you put them on. By the end of the day, body heat will cause horizontal lines and true bulges will out!

Correct short-legs-long-torso proportions with balanced choices

Diversionary tactics appear to lengthen **Y** Body Type's short legs. For example: draw the observer's eye *up* to neck and/or shoulder detailing and choose narrow skirt shapes—straight, modified straight or narrow A-shape. Or, wear short tops with set-in sleeves plus narrow, straight-leg pants and high heels. Pants must touch your instep for good proportion; keep skirt hem just below the knee. NOTE: One-value or close-value color connections work well for **Y.**

Short legs, long torso? Don't . . .

Lanky sweaters and tunics, especially with bulky sleeves, are anti-Dress Thin for **Y** proportions; so are long skirts and flounced styles. Also avoid horizontal designs and yokes on blouses and skirts (center); any short pants (right), belts, and horizontals on sweaters or tee shirts. Have pants cuffs removed.

7. Major Dress Thinvestments
Coats

If, as I do, you live in one of the "temperate" parts of the country where winter doesn't kid around, this is a chapter that can help assure the success of the most important fashion purchase you will probably make: a coat. This essential piece of clothing can cost you a lot in monetary terms—and even more in morale—if you choose one that emphasizes proportion problems rather than corrects them. Let's say that coats are a heavy subject in more ways than one.

Whether your coat is made of wool, fur, fake fur or quilting, or a lighter fabric that's just meant to keep off rain, it adds another layer to your figure. The more layers, the more weight—not just literally, but visually. That's what makes a coat almost as hard to choose in its way as a bathing suit is at the bare end of the Body/Style spectrum.

Even if the climate you live in requires only a raincoat, chances are you'll give it a lot of wear, and it still adds that problematic extra layer. So it's important to make a sleek choice, and this chapter will help you do that. Treat *any* coat like the major investment it is.

Choosing a cloth coat to help you Dress Thin. When I asked top coat designer Ilie Wacs to name the biggest potential pitfall in the coat department, he pointed out that if the price tag makes you suspect that a cloth coat you're considering is too cheap, it probably *is* cheap. Which means it can't be made of one of the soft, drapey kinds of fabric that are literally Dress Thin coat material. Nor can it be expertly tailored to fall fluidly from your shoulders to hem, without pulling into horizontal stress lines that underscore proportion problems anywhere they show up. If a coat pulls, moreover, it can't be comfortable. *Never* buy a coat that feels uncomfortable and expect to Dress Thin in it.

The best Dress Thin style choice (in fur, too) is one that skims rather than hugs the body, but doesn't envelop you in yards of (expensive!) coat fabric, either. Any style you opt for (including the tent) must fall from a close fit across your shoulders and collarbone, and none should billow or stand out stiffly. Stay with simple coat shapes, because complicated cuts are inevitably bulky and fattening. Also select the minimizing details you'll see illustrated in the pages that follow—such as vertically set buttons and pockets—and *reject* oversize collars, horizontal closures and horizontal slash pockets or bulky patch pockets.

A set-in sleeve with a high armhole is the most thinning sleeve choice and will accommodate only a dress or sweater under your coat. If you're intent on looking your thinnest, avoid layering heavy coat and suit fabrics. But, if you want to trade off for warmth, choose a coat with *dropped* armhole, set-in sleeves. Raglan-sleeve coats usually do have the necessary sleeve room to permit layering a suit, but the raglan line is broadening, especially to **r** and **b** Body Types who are heavy above the waist. It really is a good choice only for the broad-shouldered **V** body.

No matter what coat look you choose, a below-the-knee or calf-length hem will help streamline your look. A jacket will *not* give you the long, thin illusion that a well-chosen coat creates.

In addition to the style guidelines just covered, there are some tailoring fine points that are essential to your Dress Thin coat effort. In fact, you've already become well versed in tailoring if you've read my chapter on Dress Thin power play suits; a thinning coat is tailored with the same precision as a suit jacket. Watch these two essential tailoring checkpoints:

1. Shoulders deftly padded to bring the eye up, straighten the line of your back and make everything below the shoulders seem slimmer.

2. Coat closes smoothly—no gaps, and no pulling across the bust, waist, hips, thighs, back or shoulders.

The basic Dress Thin strategy for coats is: the flatter the material, the thinner you look. This applies to every coat—fur or fake fur, woollen, quilted or raincoat. If it's thin enough to move with you, you know it's thinning. If it's bulky, it will make you look bulky, like a duck with an extra layer of fat all over. Winter coat and raincoat fabric recommendations are detailed below; Dress Thin furs on page 173.

How to recognize Dress Thin coat material. You can recognize true Dress Thin coat material by its smooth (not hairy or fuzzy) surface and its drapey character. *Avoid* thick and/or stiff fabrics that inevitably create bulkiness around your body. Fabric that's tightly woven will keep you warm, but bulkiness or thickness do not *guarantee* warmth. Unless it happens to be on sale, a coat in the fabric you want has to cost a pretty penny, so when you shop be prepared to take plenty of time and make a careful choice. Study the coat illustrations designated by your Body Signs to help you zero in on styles with Dress Thin potential for your particular figure. When you read coat advertisements, watch for the fabrics recommended below for their tightly woven and drapey qualities.

Among the fibers that make thinning coat fabrics, the best—and most costly—are cashmere, vicuña and camel's hair. But you can get a thinning look at less cost by choosing a smooth coat fabric made of 100 percent wool or a blend of wool and synthetics. Fabrics to *avoid* are those made of mohair, llama and alpaca, all of which are not only very costly but also have hairy textures that visually increase your weight.

Look for the following names that describe the most thinning flat weaves that drape gracefully instead of adding bulk to your figure: flannel, gabardine, twill and melton—provided it's one of the softer meltons rather than a heavy, stiff one. *Avoid* hairy or curly textures with names like poodlecloth and bouclé. Although "double-faced" coats are interesting for their reversibility, their Dress Thin potential is low because the lamination (or the binding) that holds the two fabric "faces" together in their sandwich makes them too stiff and bulky.

In raincoats, look for poplin, vinyl and nylon—but only a thin, drapey nylon, not the stiff ones that stick out from the body. *Avoid* fitted raincoats of shiny nylon that will cause highlights on the heaviest parts of your figure. If you want a lightweight transseasonal coat, consider one of the slightly less thinning fabric possibilities, some of which may be treated to repel rain. Among these are thin-wale corduroy (seven or more "wales" to the inch) and smooth velvet—not the "crushed" kind that adds pounds visually because of its creased effect. And if you're attracted to a sweater coat, pick a medium-weight knit, not one made of hairy, fluffy yarn or one with big, heavy cables.

In both winter coats and raincoats, fabrics with *no* pattern are the surest Dress Thin material, but tiny tweeds, herringbones, houndstooth patterns and very muted, narrow vertical stripes are trade-off possibilities to consider if you're in the mood for fabric interest. I recommend that you *don't* make a heavy coat investment in such high-calorie patterns as Harris tweed, plaids, bold blanket stripes or horizontal stripes of any width.

Finally, to Dress Thin, *avoid* the bulky look of fur-lined stormcoats and raincoats. The best lining choice for *any* coat is a thin, smooth satin or taffeta. If a tag or label advertises a nonsag lining, this is an important Dress Thin asset to your coat, too.

The quilted coat trade-off. Now that you're well versed in the flat, drapey fabrics that help you dress thinner in a coat, you know that stiff, bulky fabric creates shapes of its own, instead of following or conforming to the you-shape that's inside your coat. But suppose you've developed a yen for the bulkiest coat of all—a quilted one. You're attracted to its warmth and its fun look, and you're willing to trade-off to get those qualities, instead of a more ideal Dress Thin coat look.

Well, first, here's a comforting thought: since nobody looks thin in a quilted coat, you probably won't look any fatter in one than the next person. If, however, you're an **A, b** or **T** Body Type, or if you're under 5 feet 4 inches, I recommend a long, hard look in the mirror before you buy. If the coat makes you look almost as wide as you are high, it's not a trade-off—it's a coat you'll regret.

Next, I suggest that some quilted coats are less fattening than others, so choose carefully. Before recent technological innovations in synthetic insulating fibers, goose down and duck down were warmer than the synthetics, so if you wanted big warmth, you had to have a *big* down coat. Down technology necessitated puffy, airblown rows of quilting, whereas polyester fiberfill could be sewn into comparatively thinning rows—less puffy, but also less warm. Now, however, advances in synthetic insulators make them just as warm as down; consequently your quilted coat has more trade-off potential.

Still, remember that no quilted coat can drape and conform to your body as fabric does. But if you're sold on the warmth and look of a quilted coat and you want to get the thinnest effect in that category, the ideal choice would combine:

- Synthetic filling
- Vertical rows of quilting (next best is chevron pattern)
- An unbelted style
- A coat that covers the knee by several inches (if your quilted coat looks *chopped* off, it won't be a successful trade-off)

Dress Thin furs—the classics. Famed furrier Arthur Coopchik told me that buying a fur coat is an "emotional exercise." He believes that there's a danger when buying fur of being too excited to choose rationally. With my help, though, you'll be equipped to make an investment that will pay off in warmth and flattery for years; a fur that's *you*, in a style that works for your figure. In fact, good tailoring pays dividends in fur even more than in fabric, Mr. Coopchik explained, because, "The more you wear it, the better it will fit."

Another friend and great fur talent is Pat Iuto, designer for Tepper Collection. Pat expanded on the emotional aspect of fur. "It creates psychological vibrations," she pointed out. "People are apt to be so captivated by its beauty that they are not about to notice your figure faults!" Talk about impact dressing—that's what I'd call a first-rate example. To pull it off, of course, you must know yourself inside and out, and make a choice that expresses your personality through the medium of the fur (are you a mink or a fox, hmm?)

The point is that the attraction of your fur coat should be the fur itself (or "skins" as furriers say) rather than a trendy style. To Dress Thin in fur, choose a simple, classic coat look: no fancy closures or tricky leather inserts. In fur especially—as your Dress Thin eye will confirm—coats are more thinning than jackets.

The two basic coat tailoring checkpoints on page 169 are as essential to a fur as to a fabric coat. Know them by heart before you look at a single fur! In addition, here are eight more important Dress Thin fur guidelines.

1. If it *feels* heavy on your shoulders, your fur will weigh you down and make you look heavy. If you're conscious of its weight, that's your clue that it doesn't fit properly. A good furrier tailors your coat so that *its weight is supported at the level of your collarbone*, where you won't feel it.

2. If you're under 5 feet 3 inches, a Misses size cannot be cut down to fit you correctly. Nor will a reputable store or furrier recommend such a choice. In order for it to be well proportioned for you, you must either have the coat completely retailored, or special order a Petite size. If you wear a half-size dress, your fur must also be a half-size to be properly proportioned for you. Because it takes special care to choose a Dress Thin fur, follow your body signs in this chapter with particular attention.

3. Contrary to what many women think, your fur doesn't need a great deal of "lap" at the closing to keep you warm. Fur coats may be manufactured with anywhere from 1½ to 8 inches lap, depending on the furrier, but more than 2 inches is bulky and definitely anti-Dress Thin.

4. Don't stop your fur short. Let the long, thinning line continue to below the knee or just below the top of the calf. If you're reading this book, I don't recommend a horizontally worked fur style for you.

5. Broad-shouldered **V** and prominent-bust **r** Body Types should avoid coat styles with emphasis on top—no big collars and no horizontally worked fur sleeves, for example.

6. If you're busty **(r),** don't buy a fur with upside-down V (chevron) designs that create a low-busted line.

7. If you're short-waisted **(W)** or if you're a straight-up-and-down **H** type and want to define your waist, choose a vertically worked, A-shaped style. Since it skims the body rather than hugging, this silhouette is also a good balancer for you if you're a curvy **X** Body Type. To hide the **b** type's tummy, the **W**'s short waist or to camouflage a wide waist **(H, T),** pick a straight or tent-style fur.

8. I've never seen a belted fluffy fur that was thinning, *except* when the belt was worn tied around the neck like a long, thin scarf. However, unless your Body Type is **b, r, T** or **W,** a *flat* fur coat with a neat belt is among your viable options.

Above all, remember this all-important Dress Thin fur maxim: *the flatter the fur, the thinner it will make you look.* Realize that the hairs of a coyote's fur remain the same length no matter whether the skins are made into a size 6 coat or a size 14. So if you're short—under 5 feet 3 inches—a coyote or other fluffy fur just can't be in *proportion* to your stature.

Here's a list of widely available furs, starting with the flattest and getting fluffier, to guide you to the right furs for your proportions.

1.	Russian Broadtail	13.	Mink
2.	Broadtail	14.	Stone marten
3.	Mole	15.	Sable
4.	Ermine	16.	American raccoon
5.	Persian lamb	17.	Japanese raccoon (Tanuki)
6.	Alaska seal	18.	Russian raccoon/Finnish raccoon
7.	Sheared nutria	19.	Red fox
8.	Nutria	20.	Silver fox
9.	Opossum	21.	Blue fox
10.	Sheared beaver	22.	Lynx
11.	Beaver	23.	Coyote
12.	Fitch		

Of course, I realize that one can fall in love with a fur coat that's not a sensible choice, just as one can lose one's heart to a man who might not be the most sensible choice, either. I can't offer any tips on how to handle the man, but there is a compromise strategy you may consider if you're in love with lynx (for instance) even though you know you should buy Persian lamb. This only works, however, if you're having your coat made by a furrier. In that case ask him to show you a range of lynx skins, and to help you pick out those that are the flattest, so that your coat will have the least possible bulk when it's finished. (Don't be surprised, though, if your furrier tells you that your lynx is of lesser quality than it would be if you chose really fluffy skins.)

Fur expert Herb Fischbein of Coopchik Furs told me that another good Dress Thin fur possibility may be offered by the "byproducts"—paws or bellies—of a fur that appeals to you. Fox paws, for example, are "thinner than fox skins: the hair lies *flat*," he explained; "if it's made well, you'll look thinner in a fox paw coat than in one made of fox itself . . . the paws wear better, too." So consult your furrier—you may find that a coat made of the paws, bellies or necks of your fur preference is your Dress Thin dream come true. (Plus note: They're usually much less expensive, too.)

Thin linings. A final point, and an important one, to help you choose your Dress Thin fur: make sure it's lined in a slippery, drapey silk or synthetic taffeta or satin, rather than wool or any other textured material. A silky lining permits your coat to fall correctly, instead of causing it to cling to whatever you're wearing underneath, as a textured lining does. If it clings, the sleek style of your coat will be distorted and you'll look lumpy instead of thin.

Minimize big shoulders

A raglan-sleeve cloth or fur coat (left) cuts shoulder width for you if you're a broad-shouldered **V;** or, choose a style with lapels or a collar that subtracts from shoulder width.

Minimize full bust, lengthen short waist

For prominent-bust **r** bodies, best minimizers are: straight-line (left) or A-shaped coat with V-neckline in cloth or fur, and vertical-emphasis fur (or quilted) coat. These styles are also lengthening for your short waist if you're a **W** type. Busty and short-waisted proportion problems are also corrected by the wrap (right) with its flattering V'd closing. NOTE: Wrap-coat belt should not be wider than 1½ inches.

Broad through the middle? Don't . . .

No horizontal quilting, fur designs or closings, and no belts if you're heavy in the waist **(H, T)** and/or tummy **(b)** or short-waisted **(W).**

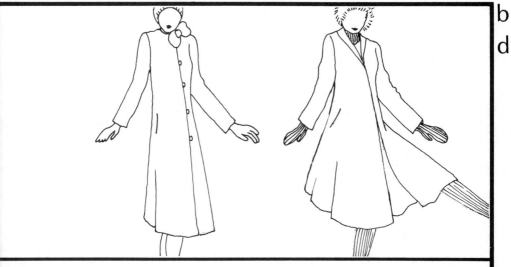

Camouflage profile proportion problems

If you're a **b** or **d** profile Body Type, you can hide prominent tummy or derrière in a body-skimming coat (or a tent style).

Solve mid-body proportion problems

If you have no waist **(H)** or a short one **(W),** shoulder detail or padding (left) in a cloth coat (or fur) provides top width that makes waist look both longer and thinner. Or, choose a fur-collared cloth style to shift the focus up.

Conceal short waist and lower-torso problems

If you're short-waisted **(W)** or heavy below the waist—in tummy **(b)**, hips or thighs **(A, T, X)** or derrière **(d)**—no one will know it if you wear a cape or poncho; notice how raised hoods, graceful folds and poncho's V'd design lengthen the bodyline. Tent style (right) has the same concealing virtues, whether you choose it in cloth or fur.

Deemphasize hips, thighs and derrière

Hips, thighs and derrière seem thinner when you bring the focus up to a Control Point above them, so if your Body Type is **A, d, X** or **T,** padded shoulders or a hood is good strategy. Hood must be nice and full for this trick to work; it works for the **d** type's derrière problem, too. Another way to fool the eye is with vertical emphasis of fur-scarfed fur coat (right).

Balancing and Control-Point strategies for hips and thighs

If you're an **A** Body Type, belt a small, fitted waist (left) as a Control Point to focus there instead of below. If you're the **T** or **X** type, a belted straight coat (right) worn bloused corrects proportion balance.

Heavy below the waist? Don't . . .

By now your Dress Thin eye can tell: for Body Types **A, b, d** and **T** no patch pockets (too bulky), no bulk-producing belts, especially in fur. Types **A, b** and **T** should avoid horizontal slash pockets. Camouflaging and proportion-correcting coat styles are on pages 178 and 179.

Heavy below the waist? Don't emphasize it . . .

Types **A, b, d** and **T** should avoid upside-down V's (chevrons) and horizontals in quilting or fur since all these emphasize lower-torso weight. Also avoid dolman or raglan sleeves—their fullness echoes heaviness below and makes you look dumpy.

d

Too much derrière? Don't . . .

If your Body Type is **d,** a straight coat reveals your derrière—and a belt only compounds the problem. An inverted back pleat (right) is also a mistake. (See derrière-minimizing and camouflaging coat techniques on pages 178 and 179.)

Verticals lengthen short legs

Vertically worked quilting or fur lengthens the **Y** Body Type's short legs. If you're a **Y,** another lengthening coat tactic for you is a high, stand-up collar (right). For your proportions, your coat hemline should fall between two inches below the knee and the bottom of your calf curve.

Short legs? Don't . . .

Pronounced horizontal styling elements like these make everyone look heavier, but are especially unfortunate choices for the **Y** type's short legs/long torso proportions.

8. Dress Thin to Win
Active Sportswear

I f I hadn't been an avid skier and tennis player, I might never have been inspired to go beyond the scarves, jewelry and fabrics that launched my design career. But when I began playing tennis and couldn't buy an outfit anywhere that was both flattering and comfortable, I was especially absorbed by the question of how a player's clothes affect her game—and her opponent.

Obviously, freedom of movement is crucial, and I realized that just *being in motion* makes you look thinner, which is a good start! I suspected that with a little streamlining, clothes could reinforce that basic advantage. I also noticed that the better I looked, the better I felt—and the more likely I was to win. (As a beginning tennis player, I needed all the help I could get.)

When I made my first tennis outfit, I designed it to emphasize my Control Point—small waist—and minimize my derrière and thighs. I was still a beginner, remember, but once I started playing in my own design . . . I never seemed to have a problem finding a partner. Even if I didn't win, let's say I definitely improved my form! And by choosing well, you can, too (as you already know if you've bought a bathing suit with the help of my swimwear chapter). What's more, you can do it in anything from weightless little running shorts to maximum-coverage Dress Thin ski clothes—all of which, and more, are illustrated in this chapter.

Dress Thin geometrics. Unique to active sportswear (bathing suits included) are the geometric elements that in themselves have tremendous Dress Thin potential, *if* you know how and *where* to wear them. I've learned lots about this strategy from watching gymnasts and designing their leotards. Someday, I'm going to figure out exactly the right place on the body to put a geometric that actually will *hypnotize* the opposition, but in the meantime let me show you some geometric tricks that will help your Dress Thin score the minute you bring them into play.

Whether you're running, biking, skiing or playing tennis—even golfing—one of the fastest proportion-streamliners you can wear is the sidestripe. Whether

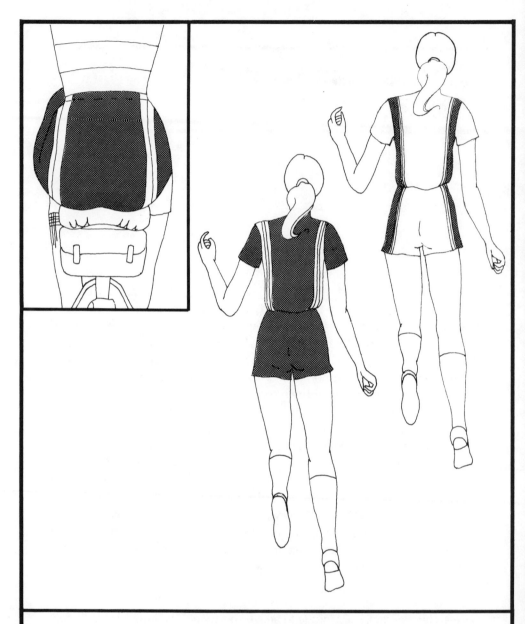

The Dress Thin sidestripe

Based on your Body Type, play with sidestripes to create better balance: if you're heavy *below* the waist **(A, b, d)**, short-legged **(Y)**, or wide-waisted **(H)**, choose wide white stripes on dark shorts (or ski pants or warm-up pants).

If your proportion problem is width *above* the waist **(r, V)** or you're short-waisted **(W)**, equalize with wide white sidestripes on dark tee shirt (or ski parka). This combination works for a wide-waisted **H**, too. To help straighten curves if you're an **X** type and to balance **T** type's heavy torso-thin legs proportions, wear sidestripes on *both* top and bottom.

you wear it on your shirt (or parka) or on your shorts (or ski pants) depends on your Body Type. If you're short-legged (Y) or your heaviness is below the waist (types A, B and d) sidestripes appear to shave pounds right off and lengthen your line.

If you're busty (r), short-waisted (W), or broad-shouldered (V), lighten and lengthen your upper torso with a sidestriped top. You can wear sidestripes on *both* top and bottom to streamline your whole torso if you're a curvy X, or a torso-heavy T. See how the sidestripe works in the illustration opposite.

Equally effective for *every*body who wants to Dress Thin, but not always as easy to find on the sportswear racks as the sidestripe, is the torso-slimming diagonal slash, an illusion tactic that breaks up torso width, narrowing and lengthening your bodyline for a leaner total look.

If you're narrow above the waist and wide below (A) or if you're small-breasted (i) but have a tummy (b) or derrière (d), a down-pointed chevron geometric or contrast color on the shoulders of your tee shirt or parka creates good proportion-balance. *Don't* emphasize hip width with an upside-down chevron or with horizontal stripes or a broad horizontal logo on your top. Of course, no horizontals on shorts, ever!

Streamline your sports form with color. It doesn't matter how much or how little you're wearing; either way, you can exploit the unifying effect of color to make you look fast and lithe. All covered up on the ski slopes or in a sweatsuit—or stripped-down to shorts-and-a-tee, one color for bottom and top is a basic Dress Thin strategy to make you look longer and leaner. The minute you break your bodyline with contrast, you cut height and risk adding pounds.

There is a way you can use contrast to *reinforce* the lengthening effect of your one-color strategy, however, and that's by wearing contrast at sleeves or neckline, to bring the observer's eye *up*. To use this trick on the tennis court, rev up your white tee shirt with bright sleeves *unless* you're busty (r) or broad-shouldered (V), and if you're either of those types, then get a tee shirt with contrast-color neckline trim or collar. Either way, your shorts should be white, too, of course.

Against the snowy white slopes, dark pants plus a dark parka with light or white sleeves will leave you looking almost as narrow as a ski, because your arms will blend into the background, letting the observer's eye travel straight along your legs and body with no horizontal to accentuate width. (Watch out for pocket horizontals—see my suggestions about pocket styles and placement in the illustrations later in this chapter.)

Dress Thin tee shirt points. Little details can make big improvements in how you look, and I maintain that if you look like a winner, you're apt to be one. If the five minutes you spend on your eye makeup when you dress for sports are worthwhile, so are three minutes in front of the mirror to consider whether your tee shirt gives you more Dress Thin points if you wear it outside your shorts or tucked in. . . .

If your proportion problem is in the middle of your body—short waist (**W**), tummy (**b**) or no waist (**H**)—wearing your tee outside your shorts is a good camouflage tactic. If you're busty (**r**) or broad-shouldered (**V**), you get better balance with your tee worn out. But for wide hips or thighs (**A**), a substantial derrière (**d**), or short legs (**Y**) the best proportion balance occurs with your tee tucked in.

Depending on your Body Type monogram, you may have to choose the lesser of two evils. For example, if your initials are **Yr,** you can't simultaneously camouflage bust with your tee worn out *and* lengthen your legs with it tucked in! The way to resolve this sort of conflict is to use the Squint Trick and let your Dress Thin eye and your mirror tell you which option gives you the *longest line.* In the example I just gave, the answer will depend on whether your legs or your bust are the dominant proportion problem—just take a good squint and you'll quickly find out.

Dress Thin shorts subjects. If you play tennis or run and are heavy below the waist (in the thighs, especially), you'll feel a lot more confident knowing you've chosen shorts that are as minimizing *and* as comfortable as possible. Some hot tips on how to recognize shorts that fit that description come from Nina Kuscsik, the effervescent world class runner and women's winner of the Boston and New York Marathons.

"An 'easy' fit, the right leg length and the right length in the crotch, are the keys to a streamlined look and comfortable fit in shorts," says Nina. "You don't even have to be overweight to have bulges on your upper, outer thighs, but they won't show as much if you make sure the length of your shorts just covers the bulge," she explains. And if you have *any* lower-torso heaviness, "It's so important that your shorts not hug these bulges. Tight shorts usually chafe, and bulges and wrinkles can't help but make you look fat!" See the illustration (below) of this technique.

"Have you ever noticed how some runners' shorts ride up and show a lot of rear end? Not very Dress Thin," Nina points out. When that happens, it's because shorts aren't long enough in the crotch. To avoid this problem and for all-round comfortable shorts fit, here's the fitting room technique that Nina developed and uses to test all the running gear that sportswear manufacturers send her:

"Just because your clothes look good when you're standing *still* isn't enough. Do a little jogging in place, and *do it with your eyes closed.* This will let you experience what your *body* experiences as comfort, and not just what pleases your eye. You'll *feel* it right away if your shorts aren't comfortable in the crotch, and if your tank top binds under the arm. Double check for correct crotch

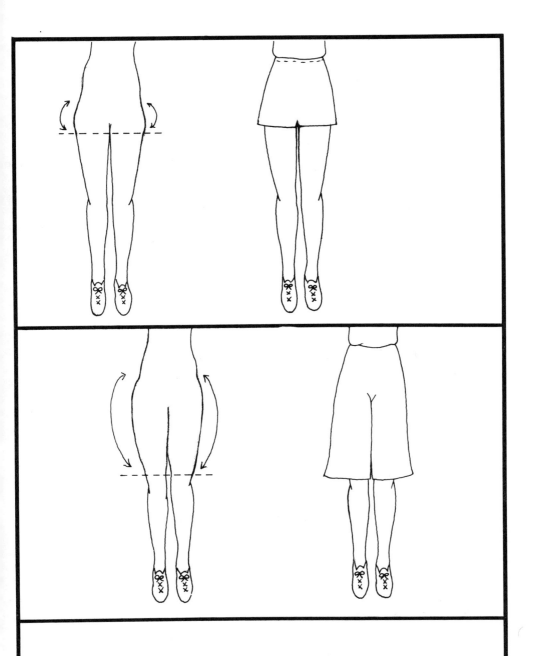

The right length for your active sportswear

If you're an **X** or an **A** Body Type with bulge(s) on the outer or inner upper thighs, your tennis skirt or tennis, running or biking shorts should end just *below* wherever the bulge ends, as shown in the top illustrations. If your legs are more uniformly heavy or flabby (below), a longer hemline wins the most points for flattery. Golf skirts, bermudas and culottes are all perfectly acceptable on the tennis court! To keep your legline as long as possible with longer-hemline sportswear, add foot socks—not anklets—to your sports shopping list.

length by looking at yourself from the back, too—keep jogging!—do the shorts ride up? Now triple check by sitting down in them. Are they still comfortable?"

Will you find a Dress Thin winner in the army-navy store? Most Body Types won't find a flattering fit in surplus stores or campus bookstores either. Army-navy style sweatshirts, sweatpants, running shorts and what-have-you that are cut for men's proportions just cannot be expected to correct yours. For instance, shorts and pants for women are cut proportionately longer in the crotch than are men's. And though you may pay less for army surplus tops, what you'll usually get is a lot of surplus fabric that won't do a thing for your Dress Thin score. If you're a straight-up-and-down **H** Body Type, there's a chance you'll find happiness in an army-navy style, but, in general, women are better off buying active sportswear that's made for women. The places to find it are pro shops and active sportswear departments.

Fabrics that play along. No matter what sport you want to Dress Thin for, your options are likely to include stretch fabric in some form—usually knitted, sometimes woven. Their obvious advantage is that they move with you; often, however, a disadvantage is that they cling to every curve and reveal every bump. The warm-up outfits or sweatsuits that are so essential to most sports almost invariably seem to be made of knit fabrics that show every bulge. If you have any lower-torso proportion problem, therefore, these outfits are basically anti-Dress Thin.

Fortunately, however, there are ways you can counter the disadvantages of knit fabrics in warm-up wear. First, choose a flat-knit suit, rather than one made of a pile fabric such as terry or velours. Then pick an outfit with a jacket that comes down past the widest part of your hips instead of one that stops at the waist. And lastly, get your suit in a dark, cool color such as navy or forest green, ideally with shoulder-emphasizing geometric detail to direct the eye *up*. If you're a runner, consider not wearing warm-up pants at all! A good substitute that will camouflage thighs is a pair of properly cut dark shorts (see the Style Guide for examples) worn *over* dark *tights*. And if you're a tennis player, *don't* add ten pounds to your hips by tucking the skirt of your tennis dress into your warm-up pants.

Speaking of warm-up wear and its disadvantages, skiers who are heavy below the waist have a lot to contend with in insulated warm-up pants. My suggestion here again is: stick to a dark, cool color. In addition, look for synthetic insulation rather than down—it's usually less bulky. The same goes for insulated ski parkas: if you're heavy *anywhere* in the torso, *don't* wear one of those old-style down-filled jackets that look like potato sacks. Be aware that the thickest insulation isn't necessarily the warmest, and that the newer synthetic insulations equal the effectiveness of down.

When choosing a nylon ski shell or parka, look for fabric that's supple and drapey rather than stiff, and subject your choice to this little test . . . crush the fabric in your fist, then open your hand and see whether the fabric forms sharp, pointy creases or rounded ripples: nylon fabrics that ripple have the Dress Thin advantage because they won't stand out stiffly from your body, adding bulges where you have none.

For spring skiing, body-skimming classic pullover sweaters in dark colors are a good choice for a busty **r** Body Type because these sweaters are tightly knitted and thick enough so that they don't cling to your curves; just be sure not to pick a sweater with bust-emphasizing geometric detail! The relative softness of a sweater shape as compared to a parka makes a sweater a good choice for a straight-up-and-down **H** Body Type, too. The ideal one for you if you're this type would have geometric detail at shoulders to broaden shoulders and so make your waist appear smaller.

What about ski pants fabrics? It's hard to beat the freedom of movement you get in fabrics made with elastic fibers, and these also have the advantage of not adding bulk. But if your proportion problem is below the waist, be sure to check the Style Guide diagrams for optimum Dress Thin styling of stretch fabric pants.

Even ski *underwear* fabrics make a Dress Thin difference. Underwear knits with elasticized fiber are better choices than all-cotton knits because their stretchiness not only offers freedom of movement, but also the clingy fit you need for a smooth line, unmarred by bunching. If you prefer nonelasticized fabrics though, make sure your long johns fit *well:* no baggy crotch or extra fabric anywhere to cause bunching under your ski clothes. And not too tight, either—that makes your underwear creep down.

Finally, if you run, bike or play tennis, all you need are well-cut shorts, but here, too, fabric can help make your shorts Dress Thin winners. In tennis shorts, for example, woven fabric skims over any bulges but does hold horizontal creases and smile lines at the crotch. So try to find smoothly tailored shorts in a substantial knit fabric (heavier than a tee shirt) which won't cling *or* wrinkle.

For running, the best shorts fabric is a thin supple woven or knitted synthetic. Synthetics allow sweat to evaporate, whereas cotton absorbs the moisture, adding unwanted weight and guaranteeing that wet shorts will stick revealingly to your curves. Evaluate the fabric's Dress Thin character with the same crush test I recommended above for ski parka fabric. For biking, if you have any lower-torso proportion problems, try to steer clear of regulation knitted bike shorts with the chamois patch on the derrière—this clingy style shows *every* bump and bulge. I promise you'll look and feel a lot racier in camp shorts or Swiss army shorts. Both are long enough to give you good derrière coverage when you ride, and both are available in sizes cut for women's figures.

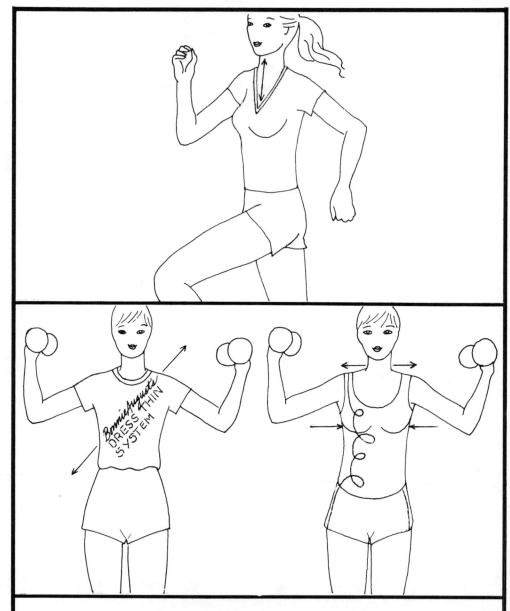

Minimize upper torso with a tee

If you're the broad-shouldered **V** Body Type or the busty **r,** Dress Thin for tennis or running in a torso-lengthening V-neck tee. Left: if you wear the logo of your favorite cause, I hope it's a low-key logo that doesn't create a heavy, eye-stopping band across your top. Short sleeves should end above the point of your breast, especially on a logo tee, otherwise a bust-emphasizing horizontal line will result. Not the ideal Dress Thin choice, but a good compromise on a hot day: tank (right) with wide-set straps that minimize by breaking up your upper-torso width.

Heavy on top? Don't . . . Small-breasted? Do . . .

Don't exaggerate broad **V** shoulders, **r** bust *or* heavy arms with cap sleeves (left); sleeveless styles; horizontal geometrics on shoulders or bust; or squared necklines. Also notice how a belted tennis dress underscores full bust. But, if you're a small-breasted **i** type or a narrow-shouldered **A**—these are all *good* proportion-correcting choices for you.

V

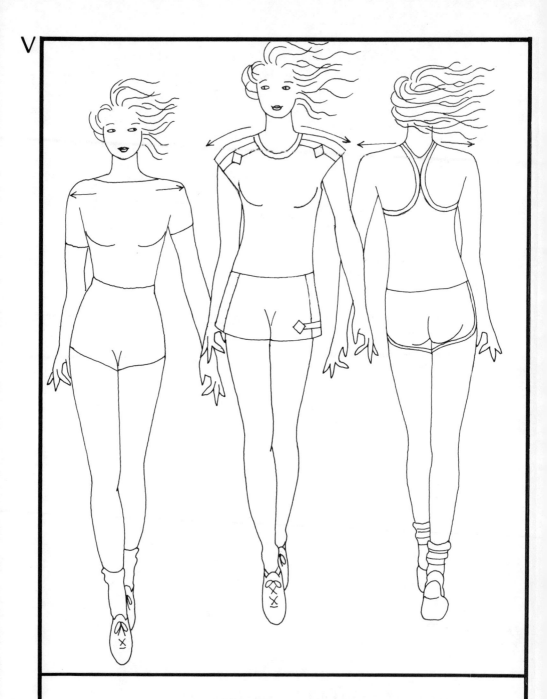

Big shoulders? Don't . . .

A broad-shoulder **V** type should avoid the boat-neck tee (left), and the extended shoulder style. Also, *don't* race in the racing-style back—it doesn't break up the broad expanse of your shoulders in rear view. Minimizing tees for you are illustrated on page 192.

Minimize prominent bust

If you're the busty **r** Body Type, you can play Dress Thin tennis with Chris Evert's strategy—a nonstretch, constructed top dress (left) that offers both coverage and good support. Or, try a Lycra spandex stretch leotard under your shorts (center)—the stretch fiber offers minimizing control. To Dress Thin for running, a dark solid-color tee works best.

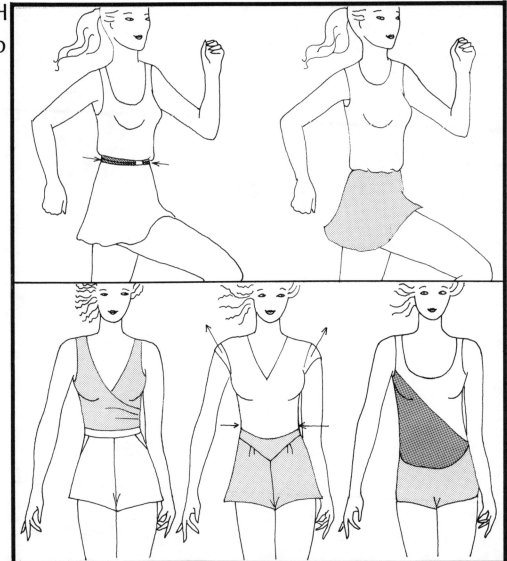

Waist and tummy-minimizing ideas for
tennis and running

H Body Type can score a waistline in a belted tennis dress (top left) provided you're not flabby in the middle. Both **H** and **b** types with tummies get Dress Thin camouflage points for a blouson dress, and a little flab can be smoothed out with a stretch Lycra leotard under shorts (bottom row, left). Notice how cap sleeves' diagonal lines persuade the eye that the waist narrows even though it really doesn't (bet you never thought of *that!*). Or how about a bold, diagonal disguise for waist and tummy problems? Make sure your running or tennis tee shirt just "kisses" the body (no hugs!) and wear it outside your shorts (bottom row, right).

Correct short waist; tummy; too-curvy torso

If your waist is short **(W),** your tummy bulges **(b)** or your relatively small waist makes you look heavy above and below it **(X),** here are three winning proportion-corrector styles for running and/or tennis: comfortably loose, hipbone-length tee, worn out; body skimming tennis dress (center); dropped-waist tennis dress.

Heavy middle or short waist? Don't . . .

For both short-waisted **W** and wide-waisted **H** types—please no horizontal stripes—especially at the waist. Don't play (or run) in a tight top that reveals bulges, or a tight dress that wrinkles across the middle. Ditto for tee-shirts stretched over bulky cut-offs or over shorts with bulky waistbands, pocket details, et cetera. . . . Look like a winner in the running and tennis gear on the two preceding pages.

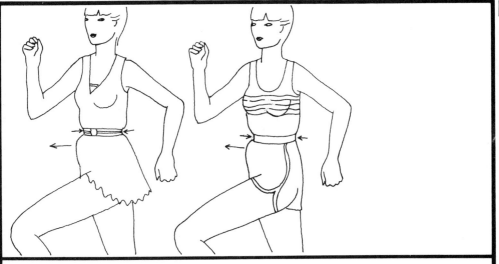

Wide waist? Tummy bulge? Don't . . .

Don't run in bulky drawstring (or elasticized) shorts (left) if you're the **b** type with tummy bulge or a heavy-waisted **H** or **T** Body Type. And why let your tee shirt bunch up around your middle when it's so easy to keep it smooth under the elastic of your panties?

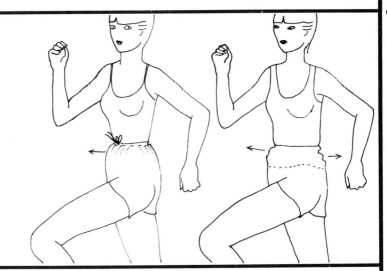

Tummy bulge? Short waist? Too curvy? Don't . . .

For good form on the courts, don't underscore tummy bulge **(b)**, short-waistedness **(W)** or extra-curvy proportions **(X)** with a belted tennis dress. You can't play well, either, if you try to squeeze into shorts with a waistband that's too tight—so don't!

199

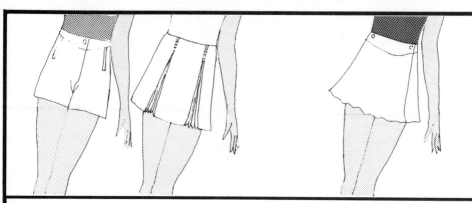

Lower-torso minimizers

Basic Dress Thin courtwear for any lower-torso proportion problem: smoothly tailored shorts (left) with vertical pockets, a flat fly, no cuffs—*nothing* to break the line or create bulk below the waist. Option 2: a pleated skirt with pleats smoothly sewn down for neat, nonbulky fit over lower torso. Option 3: swing-flare skirts such as this wrap style (right). NOTE: To create the illusion of thinner thighs **(A, X)** choose *flared* shorts, and if your legs are short **(Y),** keep the hem as high as possible without revealing any thigh bulges.

Lower-torso minimizing shorts

Most Body Types with lower-torso heaviness who bike or play golf can minimize effectively with bermuda shorts that camouflage hips, thighs, derrière, but buy them *cuffless* (or have cuffs removed) to eliminate anti-Dress Thin horizontal lines. Culottes are versatile concealers for most problems below the waist, but are not recommended proportion balancers for the **T** Body Type's heavy lower torso and thin legs, or for the **Y** type's short legs.

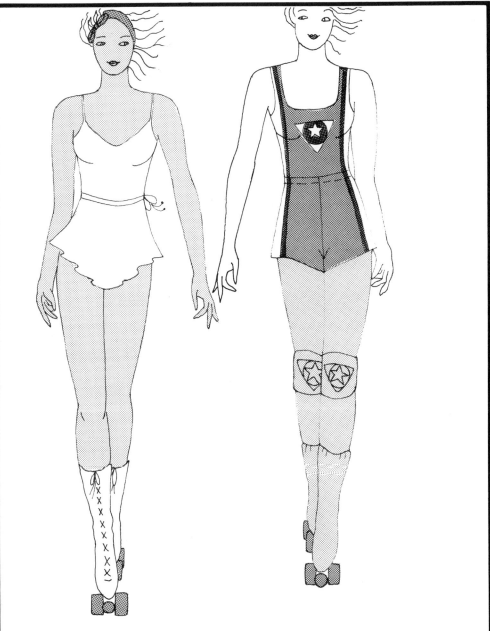

Good skate thigh-thinners, leg-lengthener tricks

If you skate regularly (roller or ice), chances are your thighs show it. Skate thin as the pros do with a flare skirt that dips in front and back to cover both inner-thigh and derrière curves. If you wear shorts, make them the same color or color-value as your tights to lengthen your legs; the final professional trick—boot covers to carry your color strategy right down to your toes.

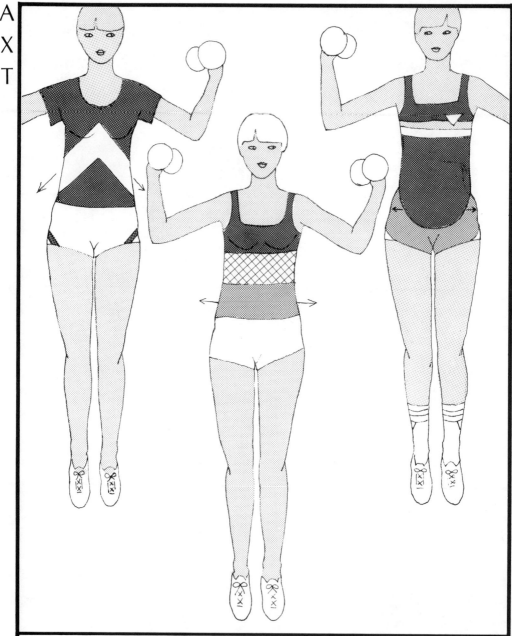

Heavy hips or thighs? Don't . . .

A, T and **X** Body Types should not exaggerate wide hips and thighs with tee-shirt designs like these, or with shirttail scallops that outline the problem. Instead, Dress Thin with a side-striped tee (see page 186), or a tee in a solid color, perhaps with a neat, centered logo.

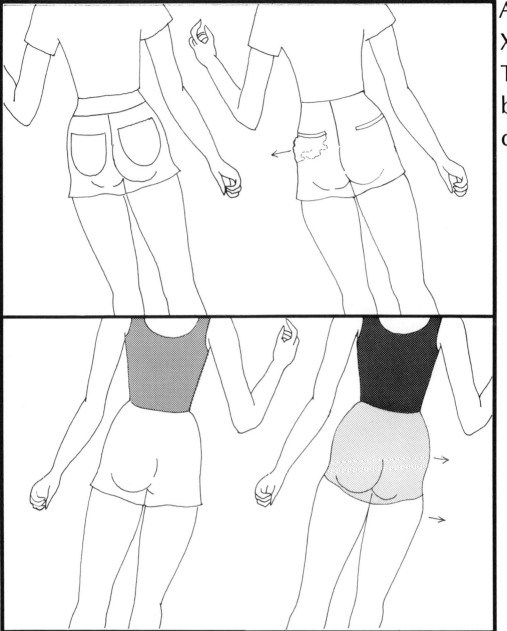

Heavy below the waist? Don't . . .

Bulky patch and horizontal pockets are anti-Dress Thin for any Body Type with too much tummy, hip, thigh or derrière (always smooth out pocket lining so pockets lie flat). Also avoid dark top/light bottom combinations that emphasize below-the-waist weight. Knit fabric shorts (bottom right) reveal all these problems—don't play with fire! See the Dress Thin winners on page 200.

203

Y

Proportion-correcting do's and don'ts for short legs

If you're a short-legged **Y** Body Type whose thighs *aren't* heavy, do lengthen legs with high-cut shorts (left) or by wearing your skirt short. *Don't* widen and interrupt legline with a dark border on your shorts or tennis skirt.

Skiwear minimizers for upper torso

The busty **r** Body Type and the broad-shouldered **V** can correct proportion imbalance by creating an unbroken line with all-in-one styling of a ski jumpsuit (left) or overalls. Be sure that belt (if any) is in the same color as the suit—and don't pull it tight. Other options: the V-neck ski sweater (*without* shoulder stripes); the tailored jacket.

Heavy on top? Don't . . . Small-breasted? Do . . .

If your shoulders or bust are big, don't fall for gimmicky ski styling—bulky patch pockets, contrast-color patches or even simple zip pockets if they're horizontal. Keep your belt easy, never tight, and especially if you're busty, avoid this booby-trap style (right). For the small-on-top **i** Body Type, all these are good proportion correctors.

Waist-minimizing ski jackets and warm-ups

Wide-waisted **H** and **T** Body Types can camouflage that problem and midriff bulge, too, with a neat loose sweatshirt or jacket (left). For skiing, narrow your waist with princess jacket styling. If you're a straight-up-and-down **H** type, you can create the illusion of a waistline with a belted jacket (right).

Short waist? Tummy bulge? Don't . . .

If you're a **b** type, don't warm-up in a sweatshirt with kangaroo or patch pockets that emphasize your tummy. Skiers with tummies steer clear of short jackets, puffy, quilted jackets and wide or tight belts that cause bulges. For a short-waisted **W** type, *no* belt at all is best. Suit up instead in Ski Thin styles like the ones on page 210.

Lower-torso minimizing skiwear

On the slopes, all Body Types with torso heaviness can Dress Thin from the inside by tucking your ski undershirt smoothly into your long johns (the least bulky ski underwear is made of stretch nylon or Lycra spandex blend; it won't ride up or bulge). Then pull on stirrup stretch pants that smooth out lower torso bulges just like control top panty hose. Or, try ski pants with ultra-thinning sidestripes. For curvy-hipped Body Types **A** and **X,** optimum tactic is a straight-leg pants style (right).

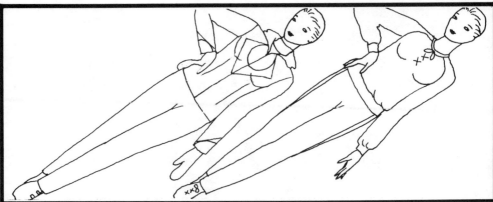

Solve tummy, hip and thigh problems
with warm-up and ski jackets

The bottom line of your warm-up (or ski) jacket can make the proportion-balancing difference if you're a heavy-below-the-waist **A, b** or **X** Body Type. The best jacket choice (left) is a semifitted style. Blouson styles camouflage the **b** tummy and hip and thigh width—for **A** and **X** types—but be sure the band sits comfortably (*not* tightly) on the narrowest part of your hips. NOTE: These are not good proportion problem-solvers for torso-heavy **H** and **T** Body Types.

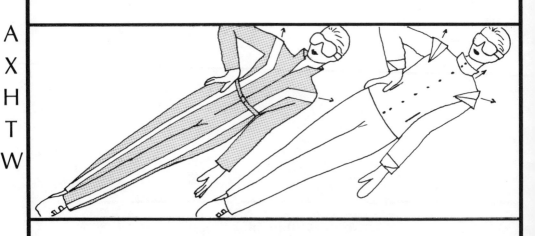

Waist-lengtheners and balancers for wide hips and thighs

To lengthen a short waist (**W**), to balance width at the bottom if your Body Type is **A, H** or **T,** and to divert attention from your curves if you're an **X** type—in each case the trick is to bring the eye *up*. Two good ways to do it are: Susie Chaffee-style jumpsuit with strong verticals ending in "wings" at shoulders (left) and jacket with wedge-shaped inserts or a funnel neck.

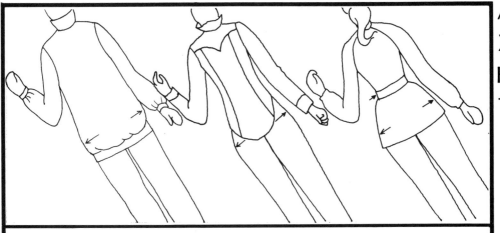

Wide hips or thighs? Don't . . .

If you're a wide-below-the-waist Body Type **(A, H, T, X)**, don't warm up or ski down in a jacket that balloons at the bottom like this (left) or one that ends in shirttails. Also avoid wide belts (maximum width should be 1 inch). Don't draw attention to lower-torso heaviness with patch (or horizontal) pockets if you're an **A, H, T** or **X** Body Type. Pick a parka like the ones on the preceding page.

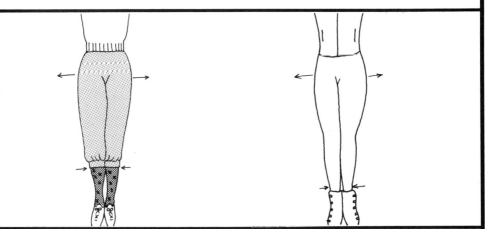

Wide hips or thighs? Short legs? Don't . . .

Don't break up a continuous body-legline by wearing socks that contrast with your cross-country ski knickers. These are anti-Dress Thin for lower-torso heaviness and the **Y** Body Type's short legs, too. And except if you're a **Y** with no thigh heaviness, avoid tapered pants because their narrow bottoms emphasize width higher up on your legs. See the leg-lengthening techniques on page 215.

d

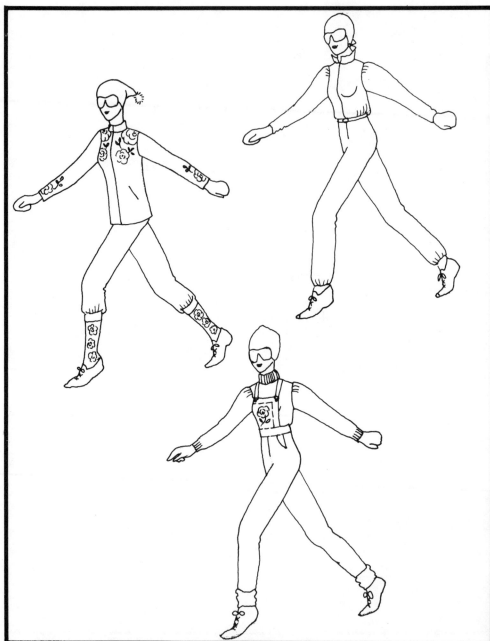

Derrière minimizers

Semifitted jacket (left) is the **d** Body Type's best Dress Thin tactic for skiing and warming-up. Notice that the jacket should be cut straight down from the shoulders in back, so it covers the top of your derrière. On the slopes, jumpsuit or overalls smooth out the **d** nicely, and blouson-back jacket effectively balances too-round rear.

Prominent derrière? Don't . . .

In choosing a Dress Thin jacket, get a style that will camouflage or compensate for—not exaggerate or reveal—your **d** type derrière curve. Very fitted, waist-length and blouson styles show it clearly; puffy quilted jacket (right) exaggerates curve by visually echoing it.

Good balance for heavy-torso-thin-legs proportions

For the **T** body, ski looks that visually balance thin legs and heavy torso: straight-leg ski pants (left) and gaiters (center). To warm-up in—gathered-bottom sweatpants (be sure to wear sweatpants long enough: to the ankle).

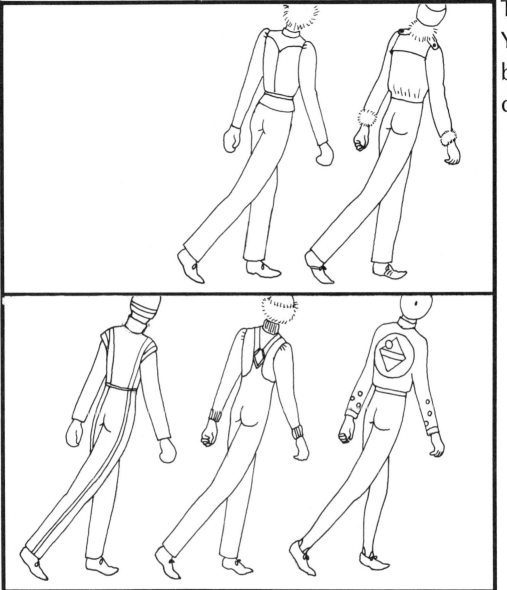

Lengthen your ski legs

There's a variety of effective options for the **Y** body who wants to lengthen her ski legs. Best pants choice: straight-legs (top); the sidestripe lengthens any pants shape. To increase the Dress Thin mileage of your pants choice, choose a leg-lengthening short jacket except if you're also a busty **r** type or have a prominent tummy **(b)** or derrière **(d).** Nothing looks leggier and lither than a jumpsuit (left). Suspender warm-up pants are also lengthening, and if your short legs aren't flabby, stretch pants with stirrups (right) are another good option. NOTE: *Always* be sure your pants meet your boot tops.

9. Dress Up Thin
Gala Clothes

Are you a Fellini fan? Do you love fantasy and costume? Has it occurred to you that a formal party offers a unique excuse to dress up, not only in a dazzling-finery sense but in the fantasy mode that children enjoy so much? Planning this chapter was perhaps more fun than any other because it brought to mind many delicious evenings when I've had the chance to project any image I chose . . . to be dramatic, surprising, outrageous, individual, flirty or vampy . . . to reveal aspects of my personality that are hidden during the day, and even during the average dinner date. If you consider that a gala occasion is your license for all this freedom of expression, *plus* an unparalleled opportunity to Dress Thin, I wouldn't be surprised if this were your favorite chapter, too.

I mentioned that spectacular dress-up clothes can also be spectacularly Dress Thin; in fact, they represent the most Dress Thin category I can think of, for three reasons: First, our now-familiar basic premise that the longer your line, the thinner you look—an idea that is perfectly embodied by the long dress. Second, formal designers frequently use sheer, floaty fabrics that, as you'll see, have exceptional Dress Thin qualities. And third: gala events permit ultra-creative, extravagant use of Control Point strategy to focus attention on whatever you consider your assets, rather than anywhere else.

A gala event, by the way, would certainly include a wedding! These three advantages are at the disposal of any bride. Those who make the most of them are destined to be the most beautiful brides of all.

The longest bodyline. You can depend on the designer to help you achieve that ultra-desirable long bodyline with any of these: a long dress, a dinner suit (long skirt or pants, plus matching jacket), a tuxedo, a jumpsuit, matching tunic and pants or pajamas . . . or you can put together a combo yourself, based on a long skirt or pants. These gala silhouettes are illustrated in detail in this chapter, with my recommendations as to which of them have the most Dress Thin potential for your Body Type. In general terms, however, it's worth noting that:

- *Any* Body Type is flattered by a long, body-skimming dress, particularly in a medium-to-dark solid color from the cool color group.

- *Upper-body* proportion problems (**r, W**) can also be optimally solved with dinner suits composed of matching jacket and long skirt or pants.

- *Lower-torso* heaviness Body Types (**A, X, H, T, b, d**) should definitely choose long skirts in preference to pants.

- *The short-legged* **Y** *Body Type* is a good candidate for pants (worn with high heels) *unless* her monogram also shows a proportion problem with hips and thighs (**A**) or derrière (**d**).

- *Anti-Dress Thin Details* to avoid are gathers, pleats, tight belts. Also horizontal pattern elements, allover large patterns, bulky or stiff fabrics.

Always indispensable, and in this case more than ever—"A three-way mirror is a woman's best friend," maintains *la grande dame* of American fashion, Pauline Trigère. "You are seen from the side and from the back, especially on the dance floor! Make sure you have previewed yourself from all angles. And you are going to put your arm around your *cavalier* when you dance, no? If he is tall and your dress has long sleeves, look and see that the line of your dress isn't disturbed when you raise your arm."

Although the long dress is the ideal gala thinner for all Body Types, I want to stress that you can ruin your entrance and the whole effect of your long formal with the wrong cover-up. In any season, a wrap is a necessity—ballrooms always seem to have built-in drafts. Carefully thought out, a cape, shawl or jacket will be lengthening and reinforce your Dress Up Thin strategy as well as the dazzle of your total look. The well-chosen cover-up is especially useful to break up shoulder width for **V** bodies and to minimize your full bustline (**r**), even if you choose a strapless style.

Having made my point about this Dress Up Thin essential, I'll show you how you can make one yourself in as little time as it takes you to sew a hem (either by hand or machine, whichever you prefer). Once you've bought your gala fashion, go to a fabric store or department store and pick out the most beautiful bolt of *sheer* silk you can find to coordinate with your formal look. My own preference is for a patterned fabric over a solid formal, but if it's a sheer, as I'll explain shortly, you can choose either a pattern or a solid for your cover-up and still Dress Up Thin. You need no more than a yard (30 to 36 inches) of 45-inch wide fabric. Take it home and hem only the nonselvage (raw) edges. Then fold it selvage to selvage and tack the opposing corners. That's all! Your custom-made designer Dress Thin cover-up is ready to go, unless you want to gild the

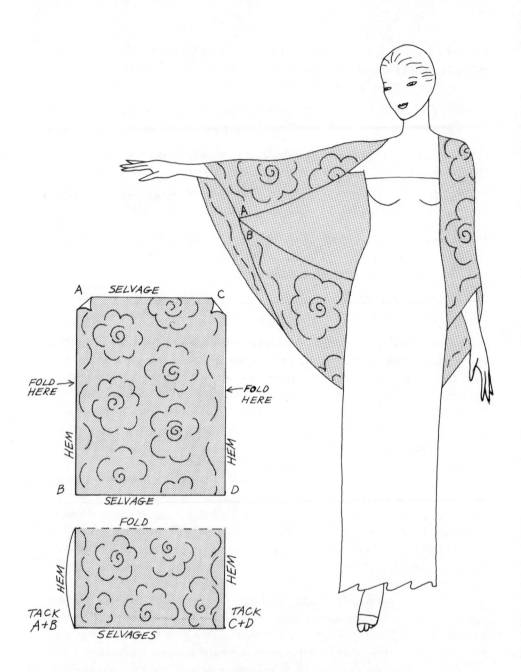

Make a gala Dress Thin cover-up—fast!

First, hem the *raw* edges of your yard of beautiful fabric. (The other edges, called selvages, are already finished.) Next, tack corner A to corner B and corner C to corner D to create the "armholes" of your gala Dress Thin wrap. That's it! (If your fabric is a solid color, consider adding pretty braid or contrast piping trim.) Notice the thinning effect of your cover-up's soft, drapey shape.

lily with some kind of pretty edging. You'll be delighted when you see how this little wisp lengthens your line while it protects you from those ballroom drafts.

Underscore your long bodyline. Now that you're on top of what goes over your formal, let's not forget what goes *under* it. You can just as easily undo all your Dress Up Thin magic and fantasy with the wrong underwear as with the wrong wrap. (To be *sure* of choosing the right undershapes—bra, bra-slip or camisole and petticoat—take your dress with you when you shop.)

Under sheer or delicate fabrics, bulky, overzealous bra constructions, distracting decorations like bows, or bumpy hardware, must all be avoided. Have a good pair of scissors and your needle and thread at the ready. Remove decorations that interfere instead of decorating; tack in bra straps that tend to slip and show at your shoulders; consider sewing your bra straps where you want them and doing away with the bumpy metal buckles permanently. If you choose lacy underwear that shows through sheer fabric or a skirt slit, make sure it's harmonious, not distracting.

Under black or dark colors, wear black underwear; beige under medium or light shades. And under slinky pants—panty line emphasizes bulges! The best way to avoid it is by wearing the right panty hose for your Body Type (see the table, Dress Thin Panty Hose Construction Recommendations, in Chapter 3).

How to float your weight away on formal fabrics. Sheer fabrics are appropriate gala material in any season, and because of their slimming character they are always my first choice. When light filters through a tissue of silk or synthetic chiffon or a crinkly crêpe georgette, *you* look lighter than you do in anything else. If you can't resist a large, flamboyant pattern for a gala, be *sure* the pattern is on very sheer fabric and you'll get away with it. . . . In my next-best category are such drapey nonsheer featherweights as silk crêpe de chine, wool crêpe, georgette and thin matte jerseys. (If mid-body flabbiness is a problem, beware of jersey; don't choose it if the mirror shows it clinging to curves you'd rather conceal.)

My third-choice fabrics include mousseline and organdy which have the desirable sheerness but are stiffer and less drapey than the sheers mentioned above. Peau de soie, surah, pongee and synthetic crêpe are nonsheer choices in this group. The drapiness of satin is in its favor, but its drawback is surface sheen that reflects light, emphasizing all bumps and bulges. Then there are the silk and rayon velvets that drape softly but have plush surface texture that adds to the width of your body.

Least desirable fabrics are those that are too bulky, crisp or stiff to make good Dress Up Thin options, such as taffeta, brocade, damask, moiré, cotton velvet, heavy lace, raw silk and allover-sequinned fabrics which are too stiff and are also shiny. Sequins and shiny metallic lamés may offer movie star glamor, but their light-reflecting surfaces make the body appear larger than it is. To my eye, a prominent tummy (or derrière) slip-covered in glitter projects more tummy than glamor!

Of course, your color and pattern choices are as important when you Dress Up Thin as they are any other time. When you're wearing a long dress, however, you may decide to indulge in a brighter or warmer color than usual. Because of the advantage you get with your long bodyline silhouette, you can afford to make this kind of Dress Thin trade-off with your formal style.

As for pattern, my little "rule of pinky" (see Chapter 1, p. 41) still holds. A confetti print, or tiny floral or dot, for instance, would be fine if you prefer not to wear a solid color. Large patterns are dangerous unless used strategically to create a special Dress Thin effect such as an asymmetric side border treatment that breaks up body width. Don't use this technique unless the mirror confirms that you've mastered it, however.

Dress Up Thin Control Point strategy. A gala event offers a perfect opportunity to use your assets to greatest effect. Focus attention on your small waist with a pretty sash or bow; reveal a pretty cleavage with the right décolletage (if you *overflow,* it's the wrong one); highlight your face with a choker, necklace or a glitter-beaded neckline—or your beautiful hair with flowers; show off good legs under a high slit skirt or a short formal hemline, neat ankles with a hemline that stops just above them rather than descending all the way to your instep.

To qualify as long, incidentally, your dress or skirt can be any length from below-the-calf to your instep. To-the-ankle offers more freedom than instep length, but both create that wonderful ultra-long bodyline. Only wear a calf-length or true short formal if fabulous Control Point legs demand it. And no matter which skirt-length nuance you choose, be sure to heed the message Pauline Trigère gave me: "No clumsy shoes!" she warned. "With a long dress, wear the highest heels you can dance in—gold or silver sandals or dyed-to-match slippers. Take special care to find a graceful shoe if your dress is calf-length or short; *never* flats."

Correct upper-torso heaviness with jacket ideas

To minimize broad shoulders **(V)** and full bust **(r),** or to lengthen your waist **(W),** wear an easy top plus a long stem of skirt. To be effective, though, both parts must have the same color background if one is a print. If so, wear the solid color on top. Possibilities include: semifitted jacket and long skirt (left); tuxedo; tunic over pants.

V
r

Heavy upper torso? Don't . . .

If you're broad-shouldered **(V)** or full-breasted **(r),** don't exaggerate upper body width with strapless, full-sleeved or sleeveless designs. Don't wear a belted style, either.

Minimize shoulders, bust; lengthen short waist

Two tactics to break up upper torso width: a deeply V'd décolletage (left); asymmetric layers of the same filmy fabric; long, graceful sleeves.

Full bust? Don't . . . Small-breasted? Do . . .

Bad strategy if you're full-breasted: ruffly or cowled bodice; high-waisted Empire line (right). If you're small-breasted, though, all three are good proportion-balancers for your Body Type.

Proportion-correctors to create a waist; balance hippiness

Width at the top corrects proportions for the straight-up-and-down **H** body and for an **A** type's hippiness: blouson bloused over a belt (left); neck-and-shoulder emphasizing detail (or padded shoulders); V'd back décolletage.

Camouflage mid-body problems

If you're a wide-waisted **(H)** or short-waisted **(W)** Body Type, or have a tummy **(b),** disguise the problem with drapey layers: several tiers of one floaty fabric (left); long tunic and underskirt that discourages bulge-revealing cling; top-of-hip-length cardigan with long skirt (or pants); pajamas + top-of-hip-length top.

Short-waisted? Tummy or derrière bulge? Don't . . .

If you're short-waisted **(W)** or have a prominent tummy **(b)** or derrière **(d),** you should wear body-skimming styles, *not* a fitted jumpsuit (left); bouffant gown (or cummerbund) or a fitted sheath dress.

A
H
T
b
d

Lighten up or disguise lower-torso heaviness

If your proportion problem is too much tummy **(b),** hips and thighs **(A),** derrière **(d)** or torso heaviness **(H, T),** sheer fabric floating around your body creates an illusion of lightness: filmy tiers (left) or panels (center) are effective also because underskirt prevents fabric from clinging to your curves. Voluminous, floaty caftan (or tent) shape is a good choice, too. Or, pick a style that breaks up heaviness below the waist with asymmetry (near left), or one that conceals it with fullness below the waist: a style with fitted bodice and full skirt (or a long A-shaped look).

Lower-torso proportion problems? Don't . . .

Whether your proportion problem is tummy **(b)**, hips and thighs **(A)**, derrière **(d)** or torso heaviness **(H, T)**, there are many good solutions in the gala category. No need even to give fitting room time to these anti-Dress Thin numbers: crystal pleating (left); narrow skirt, especially with low flare; or any kind of clingy evening pants.

Dress Up Thin tactics to lengthen short legs

Gala ideas that lengthen the **Y** Body Type's short legs include: long dresses with neck and shoulder interest and/or bustline interest plus simple skirt (left); high-waisted pants worn with high heels; bolero'd long dress; solid-color jumpsuit with straight or tapered pants plus high heels.

Short legs and long torso? Don't . . .

If you're a short-legged **Y** Body Type, gala occasions offer you special oppor-
tunities for an ultra-flattering, uninterrupted line. So scoop up a Dress Thin
design and leave these on the hanger: any belted or waist-emphasizing style;
drop-waistline or hip-emphasizing details; any street-length style.

10. Dress Thin
Control Point Theory
Accessories

I really have been saving the best for last. Anything but an afterthought, accessories are a pet subject of mine, partly because when I was just out of school, designing my own line of silk signature scarves was one of my first paying jobs. It didn't pay very much though, and at the time I couldn't afford to buy a scarf with a famous signature, let alone real gold jewelry. So instead, I often wore my own original designs, homemade of less expensive materials— jewelry fashioned from lacquered cardboard, for instance. One of those pieces, a pin in the shape of a mouth, was hand manufactured by my sister Marilyn and helped pay for her Ph.D. We both have fond memories of that collector's item and one of these days, I may do a new version in pavé rubies and diamonds. . . .

Now that inflation has made accessories so costly, even a belt is a candidate for investment spending. So perhaps women are ready also to begin investing more *thought* in accessories, and to really understand how to choose and wear them to get their money's worth.

For a start, let me suggest that your expensive handbag has a more interesting function than the one we automatically associate with it. And that the value of jewelry can be greater not only than its worth in dollars or even in sentiment (and certainly greater than its boring "status value"). Far from being the incidentals that their name implies, accessories should be compared to the *engine* of a car rather than to its hood ornament or wire wheels. A true accessory can and should run your whole look! Potentially the most important thing you wear, it can express whatever you want to say about your body and about how you see yourself in the world. It also has tremendous impact dressing potential.

What's in a handbag? In addition to holding your essentials, a handbag can both change your image and make your audience focus on whatever part of

232

your body you choose. Christine Karam, a New York photostylist who has more charisma than many of the models she dresses and accessorizes, says that even Raquel Welch would look matronly with a silly little handbag dangling from her wrist. But if Raquel wanted to be absolutely sure her breasts would be noticed before anything else—she could carry a bright red clutch bag right under her arm.

If you're a busty **r** Body Type but want to project a more intellectual image, carry a sleek attaché case in your hand. On the other hand, suppose your Body Type is **b** and you want to divert attention from your tummy—it's as easy as wearing a shoulder-strap bag that hangs at about thigh level.

One of my own best-loved accessories is a hot pink parachute-nylon bag on a leather shoulder strap. Since I wear lots of bright colors, it blends right in just as if it were a "neutral." I adjust the strap carefully so that the bag hangs near my waist, which is a Control Point that I like people to focus on. As Christine says, use your accessories to help solve your proportion problems, not call attention to them. Here are some negative examples:

Don't wear your shoulder-strap bag bouncing on a prominent rear **(d)**.

If your legs are short in proportion to your torso, don't emphasize the problem by wearing an ankle bracelet **(Y)**.

Don't wear a pendant watch that sits on your cleavage unless you want people to keep close tabs on the time **(r)**.

If you're short-waisted, don't wrap a scarf around your waist and make it appear even shorter **(W)**.

"Things like these may seem obvious," Christine says, "but everybody does them." Among the many proportion-correcting tricks in her bag is shoulder padding. "But don't wear shoulder pads in a dress or a top with a high neckline," she cautions. "The more you pad, the more you should drop the neckline to make the proportion work."

For balancing my own **X** type proportions, I often use my whole upper torso as my Control Point. Just as I was working on this chapter, I found a wonderful blouse with pearls sewn all over it. I knew I could wear it open as a jacket, tucked in as a blouse and with a zillion different things. It's a *true* accessory for all those reasons and also because when I wear it it's the most important thing I have on—the focus point. *Whatever* you use to make an attention-getting statement about yourself is an accessory: your sunglasses; the logo on your tee shirt; your gold-and-diamond choker; a bow or ornament in your hair, or your hairstyle itself.

Be especially aware that accessories worn *near your face* affect your proportions in important ways, emphasizing or playing down the relative scale of head, neck and body, as well as of your facial features. Little sunglasses or tiny earrings are out of scale if your body is big or your bone structure is heavy.

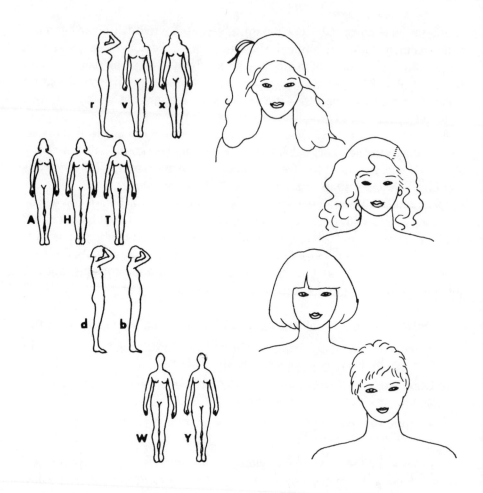

Get a head start on well-balanced Dress Thin proportions

If you're a busy or broad-shouldered Body Type (**r, V, X**), don't exaggerate your upper body bulk by wearing your hair cut very short or in a pulled-back, close-to-the-head hairstyle. A below-the-shoulders style is best for your proportions, since it breaks up the upper body (top). NOTE: If you're small-breasted (**i**), hair-shape choices are unlimited *except* if you're heavy somewhere else, so check the rest of this page for your other Body Type initials.

If you're heavy in the hips, thighs or the torso generally (**A, H, T** types), medium-length hair shape with volume is right for you. *Avoid* a small-head look that makes you seem bigger below.

Long hair brings attention to profile proportion problems for **A** and **d** types, shown third row. For best balance, your hair shape should be short and have some height (especially if your face is round). Long hair is also the wrong choice if you're short-waisted (**W**) or have short legs (**Y**), or if you're just short. The ideal for you is a short, close-to-the head style that keeps the eye going and creates an overall lengthening illusion (bottom).

Nothing, of course, is closer to your face than your hair, and your hairstyle can have an important positive or negative effect on your total Dress Thin proportion picture. In other words, think of your hairstyle as your most important accessory of all, since it's *the* one you're never seen without!

Freelance hair-and-makeup stylist Shelly Durham, who coifs and makes up top models and stars before they go on camera, says that creating the right hair shape for your Body Type can make a major difference in your Body/Style image. "There are a million articles about what hairstyle is best for your face shape," he points out, "but before I cut anyone's hair, I also always consider the proportional relationship of her head and her figure." So take Shelly's point to heart and analyze that relationship for yourself right now. To help you work out the right hair shape for you, see the diagrams on the opposite page.

The Control Point face. Both real and costume jewelry have major proportion-making Control Point potential, since all that glitters unfailingly attracts the eyes of adults just as it does those of children. When you consider a jewelry purchase, be sure you're going to wear it on a part of you that you want your audience to notice right away. Also, study the relationship of your earrings, necklace or pin to both your overall body scale and to your features. "Jewelry must not be just sculpture," says avant-garde precious jewelry designer Janice Savitt (whose sister, Michelle, you met earlier in this book). "It must complement your features."

Sister Wynne Savitt, another partner in their firm, showed me how the difference of only an inch in the length of a choker can either lengthen a round face or shorten a long one. So whether your choice is an African tribal piece or a gold bauble, if your neck is short and/or if your upper torso is heavy (**r** or **V**), wear your choker longer—resting at the *base* of your neck. To make a long face seem shorter, wear your choker higher on your neck. Wynne went on to suggest that if your facial features are delicate "but you're not so delicate somewhere else, work with what you have: concentrate on your face and your overall image will benefit." In other words, *create a Control Point with your face. . . .* Try important earrings, a beautiful necklace or an unusual hair ornament. If your hands are pretty, wear a silver cuff bracelet on each wrist. Keep clothes simple and let your hands and face express your personal Dress Thin Control Point theory.

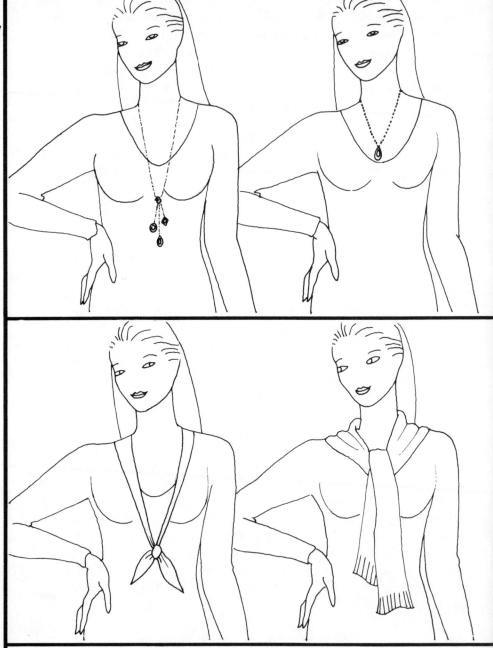

Minimize upper torso, lengthen short waist

Just as with blouse and jacket styling, a V-shape created with accessories lengthens the top of the body for a broad-shouldered **V** Body Type and a full bust **(r)**; it lengthens a short waist **(W),** too. Necklaces, scarves, even a strategically tied sweater all work the same way.

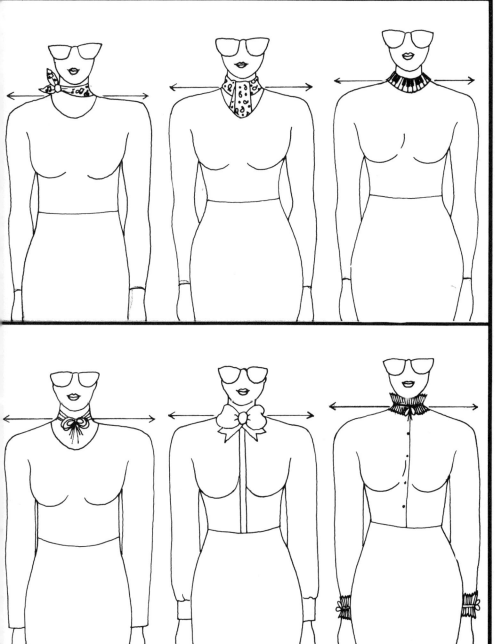

Full bust? Broad shoulders? Don't . . .

If your neck is short or if you're broad on top, don't do any of these scarf tricks or wear accessories that are tight around the neck. A small neck makes the area below it seem bigger. See the preceding page and the following one for minimizing accessories.

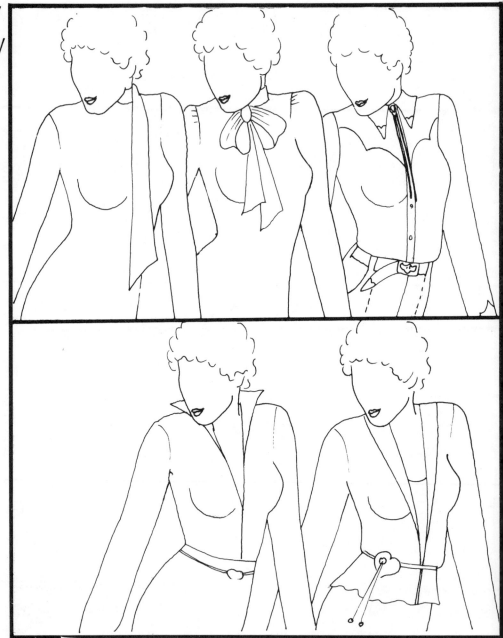

Upper-torso minimizers and waist lengtheners

Vertical line of long scarf cuts width of shoulders **(V)** and bust **(r)**, lengthens a short waist **(W)**. For those proportion problems, a closed collar should be worn with a lengthening tie, scarf or bow—and a pointed collar is better than a round one. If you're short-waisted or busty, you can lengthen by "cheating" with your narrow belt: wear it a little low, or with its *small* buckle to the side.

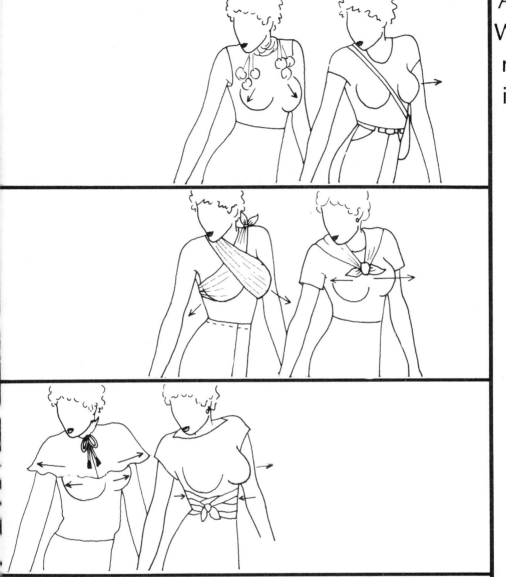

Full bust? Don't . . . Small on top? Do . . .

If you're busty **(r),** don't wear symmetrically styled necklaces (left) or heavy, thick ones that sit right on the problem. Also avoid a bag with a shoulder strap that crosses the bust diagonally defining curves. But if you're small on top **(A, i),** all of these are good maximizers.

Scarves worn as bras or halters or knotted so that they maximize you are not for busty **r** types or short-waisted **W** bodies. The same goes for shawls that create width (lower left) and the scarf-wrapped waist or any wide belt. Dress Thin accessories tactics for you are on pages 236 and 238.

Full bust or short waist? Don't focus on it

Don't draw attention to full bust **(r)** with "target" pin or pendant, or with a batch of shiny buttons. Wide belt emphasizes width above and shortens waist; clutch bag clutched under the arm does the same kinds of damage. See the minimizing scarves, belts and jewelry ideas on pages 236 and 238.

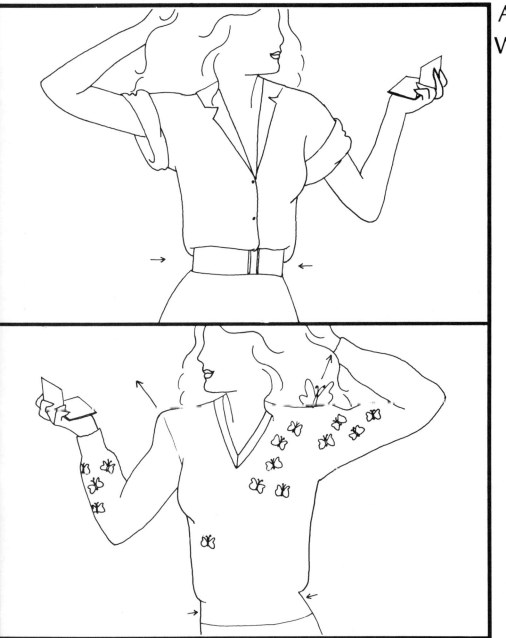

Create a waist—or focus on a small one

If you're a straight-up-and-down **H** Body Type, create a waist with a wide belt and a top bloused above it. Or, make your waist *seem* smaller by padding shoulders or by placing a jewelry statement as shown (below). These techniques also emphasize your small waist if you're an **A** Body Type (smaller above than below the waist).

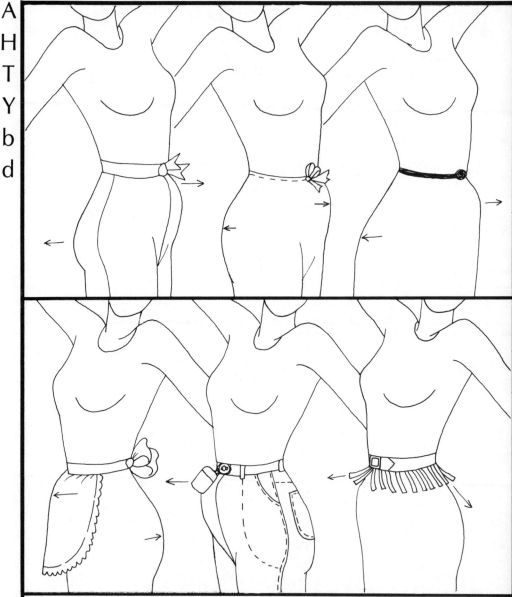

Wide waist, short legs or profile curves? Don't . . .

Would anyone with a tummy or a derrière spotlight it in one of these ways? I've seen it happen half a dozen times in a day! That's why **b** and **d** Profile Body Types (especially) must check the side-view mirror. These mistakes all emphasize wide waist **(H, T)** too. And even a narrow belt stops the eye at the waist if the color of the belt *contrasts* with skirt or pants, making short legs seem shorter **(Y)**. See the proportion-correcting accessories ideas on pages 243, 244, and 245.

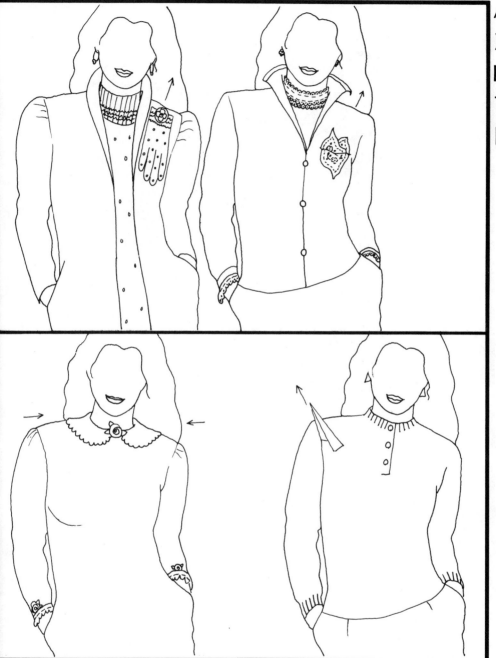

Divert attention from mid-
and lower-body proportion problems

Wide-waisted **H** and **T** Body Types and those with weight below the waist (**A, X, b**) should wear attention-getting accessories high up, as shown.

Minimizing tactics for mid-body hips and thighs

A lightweight, flippy long scarf cuts width at the waist **(H, T),** hips and thighs **(A, X, T).** When you entertain, a chef's apron is a Dress Thin recipe for hiding hip, thigh and tummy bulges **(b).** If you have a tummy, you can also hide it with a sweater tied high like this (right) *unless* you're also short-waisted **(W).**

Tie one on the beach and hide your mid- and lower-body heaviness

A pareo is a great Dress Thin beach accessory! The two tie techniques in the top row help solve any middle or low-torso proportion problems (**A, b, d, H, T, X**); the two at the bottom are good camouflage tactics for hips, thighs and derrière (**A, d, T, X**).

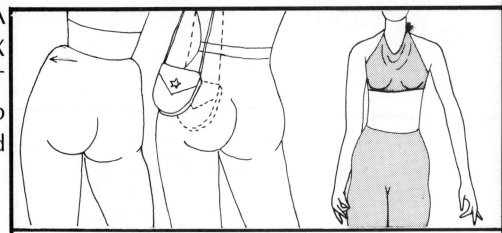

Lower-torso proportion problems? Don't . . .

Too much tummy **(b)**, rear **(d)** or hips **(A, X, T)**? Cinch belt (left) makes *every-thing* bulge. A shoulder bag bouncing on derrière **(d)**, hip **(T)** or over thighs **(A, X)** draws attention to weight there. Scarves on top aggravate problems below: for example, halter-tied scarf creates horizontal that makes derrière, hips and thighs seem wider **(A, d, T, X)**.

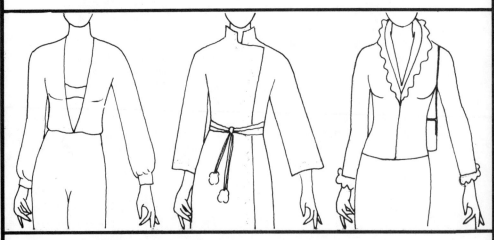

Proportion-correcting tactics for hips and thighs

Small waist but heavy below and/or above it? If you're an **A, T** or **X** Body Type, tuck in an open blouse over your strapless top to create a V-shape that balances the width below. Long skinny sash cuts heavy torso width, and helps focus on your Control Point waist if you're an **A** or an **X** type (but don't pull your belt too tight). Shoulder bag is best worn at hipbone instead of level with the problem.